MEDITATE FOR YOU

A Blueprint for Self-Care, Healing, and Opening the Heart

Dr. Anne O'Hare

ALEMBIC
PRESS

Printed in the United States of America

Library of Congress Control Number: 2025950726

Digital ISBN 979-8-9922520-3-3
Paperback ISBN 979-8-9922520-4-0
Hardcover ISBN 979-8-9922520-5-7

Published by Alembic Press
Hotchkiss, Colorado

I saw the angel in the marble and carved until I set him free
— Michelangelo

Contents

Introduction

P EOPLE DON'T USUALLY COME to meditation because everything in their life is working. They come because something has stopped making sense—the ways they've learned to cope no longer help, or they're carrying a tiredness that sleep doesn't fix. Often there's an ache that success can't touch, a quiet sense that something essential has been misplaced.

That's where most of us begin. We sit down hoping to feel better, to slow the racing mind, to soften what has become brittle. And often, after a while, we do. We begin to see our thoughts for what they are and notice what's actually happening inside—how much the mind carries, how automatically it reacts, how easily it convinces us that peace is somewhere else.

But there comes a point in spiritual practice when awareness alone isn't enough. You've tasted peace. You've learned that you are a soul, not the swirl of your thoughts. But sooner or later, you notice that the mind still pulls you back into old reactions. Emotions still rise. Peace fades as daily life presses in.

If you've reached that point, if you recognize that understanding is not the same as transformation, you're ready for what this book offers.

For years, I presented one face to the world while carrying something entirely different within. I had the education, the career, the independence. On paper, everything looked successful. Yet internally, I was exhausted. My relationships felt hollow. There was a sadness I wouldn't have admitted to anyone, least of all myself.

If you had asked me then how I was doing, I would have said, "Everything's fine." Or I would have made someone else wrong—my family, my workplace, the circumstances—so I could avoid facing what was actually happening in my own mind and heart. This went on for forty years.

The body doesn't lie. Mine told the truth long before I was willing to listen. Anxiety. Acid reflux. Chest pain. The physical symptoms reflected exactly what was happening in my mind: a constant storm I was pretending didn't exist. This is what happens when we keep trying to manage externals while ignoring what's happening internally.

But I need to be honest with you about what lies ahead: this book requires your active participation. *Meditate Anyway*, the first book in this series, gave you knowledge—concepts you could understand intellectually. This book asks you to take that knowledge and use it to investigate your own experience, to distinguish yourself from the patterns you've been identifying with, to access the benevolent nature that's waiting beneath all the accumulated layers.

Think of the first book as the freebie. You could read it, absorb the concepts, and set it down without changing anything about your life. This book is different. This book costs something. It costs your time, your honesty, your willingness to look at yourself without flinching.

This is the part of the journey where many people stop because it asks something of them. It asks for commitment, for honesty, for the willingness to look at themselves without turning away.

If you're ready for that, keep reading.

What Happens When You Begin

When I say it's time to get better, I'm not talking about improvement in the conventional sense. I'm talking about honesty. I'm talking about finally paying attention to what you've been ignoring—your actual feelings, your actual needs, the actual state of your mind.

This requires courage. It means stopping the cycle of pretending everything is fine when it isn't. It means no longer blaming others for your internal state. It means recognizing that all the external trying hasn't worked because the real work is internal.

Think about your own experience. Maybe you're the person who's always helping everyone else but never feels helped yourself. Maybe you're generous with others but harsh with yourself. Maybe you wake up determined every morning to feel better, only to find the same patterns waiting for you by noon.

The years go by this way. You keep trying. You keep hoping something will shift. But nothing does because you're using the wrong approach.

The good news is that time passing isn't punishment. It's opportunity. If you turn toward yourself now and actually start getting better, you have the rest of your life to feel better. That's worth something.

But it requires a shift. You have to put yourself first. Not in a selfish way, but in an honest way. You have to acknowledge that your mind needs help the same way a sick body needs help.

Meditation is how you assess what's actually happening in your mind. It's not about achieving peace immediately. It's about finally looking at what you've been running from.

When you sit down to meditate, especially in the beginning, your mind may go absolutely wild. Thoughts racing. Emotions churning. It feels like chaos. This is normal. This is what I call the Three-Ring Circus—everything that's been running in the background is suddenly visible.

Most people quit here. They think meditation isn't working because their mind won't be quiet. But you're misunderstanding the purpose. Meditation isn't about forcing the mind to be quiet. It's about observing what's actually there. You can't clean a house without facing the dirt.

You might be thinking: But I have decades of momentum behind these patterns. Decades of pain, sadness, negative thinking, difficult relationships. How can fifteen minutes of meditation change that?

It can't. Not immediately. But it starts something.

Think of it this way. Yes, there's a freight train of momentum behind your old patterns. But you're not trying to stop the train by standing in front of it. You're laying new track. Every morning you sit, every moment you observe rather than react, you're redirecting the momentum toward something different.

I can tell you from experience that this works. Two weeks after I started practicing meditation, anger left completely. I wasn't having peaceful experiences in meditation. I was sitting there watching the chaos. But something shifted anyway. The observation itself created change.

Over fourteen years, every aspect of my life transformed. My relationships. My health. My sense of self. Not because I forced anything, but because I kept showing up to witness what was actually there.

This work requires determination, but not the kind you're used to. Not the external pushing and achieving. This is internal courage. The willingness to sit with yourself for fifteen minutes and face what you've been avoiding.

You don't have to be good at meditation. You don't have to quiet your mind perfectly. You just have to show up and observe with mercy. That's all. The watching itself begins to create distinction.

And here's something essential to understand: this internal work isn't self-indulgent. The point of purification is to become a blessing to yourself and others. When you're no longer drowning in your own patterns, when you've distinguished yourself from the chaos, you become capable of genuine service. You can offer real help to others because you're no longer desperate for them to fix you. You can bless the world because you've stopped requiring it to heal you first.

There is no better time than now to start. The world will continue offering unlimited things to focus on other than your mind and heart. It always has. You have to decide that you matter enough to turn inward. That your internal state deserves the same attention you've given to everything external.

The Journey You're Beginning

In the first book, you were still identifying primarily as your sanskars—your personality patterns, your conditioned responses, your accumulated impressions. You were a bundle of sanskars trying to experience something different. You practiced saying "I am a soul" and perhaps felt moments of peace or clarity. But fundamentally, you remained identified with the patterns.

This book pulls you to the other side of that equation. Here, you learn to become the soul witnessing the sanskars. You develop the capacity to look at your patterns and clearly recognize: *I am not that. I am the consciousness observing it.*

When you can observe a pattern without becoming it, the pattern doesn't necessarily disappear, but it loses its power over you. You stop suffering from it. The triggers that once controlled you become simply phenomena you can watch with curiosity and clarity.

This shift, from identified to witnessing, is the work of this book. And it requires a specific structure.

Your Practice Framework

Think of this book as a 15-20 week intensive (depending on your pace). Each chapter is like a mini-workshop. Here's the framework:

Morning Meditation: At least 15-20 Minutes Daily

This is non-negotiable. Every morning, before you begin your day, spend at least 15-20 minutes in meditation practice.

I've provided playlists (Release Your Wings and The Spiritual American's guided meditation series). Choose whichever ones you're drawn to—you need some freedom in this process—but the practice itself is essential.

This daily practice reinforces your spiritual identity. It's how you tell your intellect: I am not the mind. I am the consciousness aware of the mind. Without this daily practice, the intellectual understanding remains abstract. With it, you begin to experience the distinction directly.

Week One: Read Section One Completely

Don't pace yourself on the first section. Read it straight through. This introduces you to the concept of the daily routine and sets the foundation for everything that follows.

Weeks 2-15+: One to Two Chapters Per Week

Each subsequent chapter explores either a specific sanskar (anger, overwhelm) or an environment that triggers sanskars (work, relationships, family). Treat each as its own workshop:

- Read the chapter carefully

- Work with the contemplation prompts (journal your responses)

- Spend the week (or at least a few days) observing yourself with mercy

- Notice when the sanskar appears

- Practice witnessing it rather than becoming it

Some chapters you'll revisit multiple times. This isn't a race. You're learning to see more of the sanskar each time you return. The first time through a chapter on anger, you might see only the most obvious explosions. The second time, you notice the subtle irritation that precedes them. The third time, you recognize the thought patterns that create the irritation. Each pass reveals more.

What Makes This Work Different

This is not about self-improvement in the traditional sense. You're not trying to become a better version of yourself. You're learning to distinguish the self—the soul—from everything you thought was you.

The sanskars aren't bad. They're just not you. And when you can see them clearly, when you can observe them without identification, they naturally lose their grip.

Discovery. Distinction. Discernment. These are your tools.

Let me be clear about what this means: you are not an equation being solved. You're not broken. You don't need fixing or improvement in the way most self-help promises. What you need is clarity. You need to see what's actually there, distinguish yourself from what you've been identifying with, and recognize the benevolent nature that's been present all along.

The process is firm but merciful. You're not attacking yourself. You're getting curious about yourself. You're investigating with the genuine interest of someone who wants to know: what is actually true here?

This investigation requires honesty. Not the harsh, judgmental kind, but rather the clear, merciful kind. You're learning to see your patterns without condemning yourself for having them. You're watching the way a scientist watches: with interest, with precision, with genuine curiosity about how this particular mechanism works.

What to Expect as You Work

In the beginning, you'll mostly notice patterns after they've already happened. You'll react with anger, and an hour later think: "Oh. That was the sanskar." This is normal. This is the first stage of discovery.

As your practice deepens, you'll begin to notice patterns as they're happening. You'll feel the anger rising and simultaneously recognize: "This is the sanskar appearing." You're both experiencing it and observing it. The distinction is beginning.

Eventually—and this takes time—you'll notice patterns before they fully activate. You'll see the situation that would normally trigger anger, and instead of becoming angry, you'll watch the impulse arise and pass without identification. The sanskar has lost its power because you've fully distinguished yourself from it.

This progression isn't linear. Some sanskars you'll distinguish quickly. Others will take years of patient observation. And that's fine. You're not racing toward some finish line. You're developing a capacity—the capacity to witness yourself with clarity and mercy.

As you practice, you'll notice patterns you couldn't see before. You'll recognize thoughts that have been running automatically for years. You'll feel emotions you've been suppressing. And gradually, you'll experience something

9

remarkable: these patterns will still appear, but they won't control you the same way.

Why? Because you've distinguished yourself from them. You are the soul. The patterns are something you're observing, not something you are.

Tips for Success

- **Don't overdo it.** This work requires sustained attention, not force. If you push too hard, you'll burn out or become harsh with yourself. Neither serves the investigation.

- **Trust that your intellect will pick up what you need to see.** You don't have to force insights or manufacture breakthroughs. Keep practicing, keep observing, and the distinctions will emerge naturally.

- **The suffering decreases as you distinguish.** Each time you clearly see "this is not me," you free yourself a little more. The pattern might still appear, but you no longer suffer from it the same way.

- **Watch without judgment.** Merciful self-observation means seeing clearly without condemning. When you notice a pattern, the response isn't "I'm terrible for having this pattern." The response is "Interesting. This is what's happening," and soon it becomes, "I see where this came from and how it has affected me and my life...of course I have been that way." The process continues to stimulate deeper levels of self-compassion, understanding, and freedom.

- **Your mind will get louder before it gets quieter.**
  This is normal. You're not failing meditation—you're finally seeing what's been there all along.

What Awaits You

You are working toward your own benevolent nature. Not creating it, because it's already there. But accessing it. Awakening it. Learning to experience yourself as someone capable of genuine compassion, kindness, and love that doesn't depend on circumstances.

This is spiritual self-respect: the recognition of your own benevolent capacity, independent of external validation.

Most people think self-respect comes from achievement, from doing good things, from meeting certain standards. But that's ego wearing a spiritual mask. Real self-respect—spiritual self-respect—comes from recognizing your own benevolent nature. It comes from experiencing yourself as fundamentally kind, fundamentally loving, fundamentally capable of compassion. Because that's what you actually are when you're not identified with the sanskars.

Ultimately, you can't feel real love, for yourself or others, while lying to yourself. Truth is the pathway to love. The honesty this book requires, the clarity you develop, the distinctions you make—all of this creates the conditions for love to emerge naturally.

The love I am talking about here is the kind that shows up as genuine compassion for others because you've stopped needing them to be different than they are. The kind that shows up as real kindness to yourself because you've stopped trying to be someone you're not.

This is what spiritual transformation actually looks like. Not becoming someone new. Not fixing yourself. Simply clearing away the blocks to your own benevolent nature—which was always there, waiting.

Support Along the Way

You can reach me if you need guidance. I've been on this journey. I know what it asks. If you find yourself genuinely stuck, if you need clarity on a practice or a concept, reach out.

You might also explore your local Brahma Kumaris center for community support. Raja Yoga is a path that benefits from community, from others walking the same investigation.

The meditation resources are available on YouTube through Release Your Wings and The Spiritual American Podcast. Choose practices that resonate with you. But remember: the most important practice is showing up for meditation every morning for at least 15-20 minutes, reinforcing your spiritual identity, and training your intellect to distinguish.

You do matter enough to turn inward. Your internal state deserves the same attention you've given to everything external. And the moment you begin, everything changes.

Definition of Terms

Bhavna: Deep and pure feelings in the soul.

Bodiless Stage: Inner experience of existence while completely separate/free from the influence of the body, memories of matter, time, and any time-based identity or experience.

Intellect: Aspect of the soul's inner world that has three primary functions; evaluation and decision-making, reinforcement of beliefs held by the soul, and assignment of identity.

Maya: The mind-created world/reality based on memories and emotions from past experience. When the soul's attention is drawn to this phenomenon, the soul is no longer responding to the present moment but living in illusion. Maya = illusion.

Meditation: The practice of bringing one's attention to the non-physical realities of the self, of existence, while also developing the capacity to observe the mind.

Mercy: Elevated feelings toward something. Combination of love, understanding and detachment (attention without the feeling of direct involvement)

Mind: The non- physical field of experience for the soul. Includes thoughts, feelings, emotions, ideas, images, and memories.

Raja Yoga: The connection and transformational relationship between the individual soul and the Supreme Soul resulting in purification of the individual soul and emergence of God-like qualities such as pure love, mercy, pure self- respect, and benevolence.

Sanskars: Complex patterns of concepts, perceptions, beliefs, knowledge, and experience that arise according to circumstances.

Soul: Unique living consciousness

Supreme Soul/ God: Unlimited, unique living consciousness. The unlimited source of elevated qualities such as Love, Peace, Purity, Benevolence.

1

Starting the Journey Within

The Secret of Self-Care

W E CALL OURSELVES BY many names: mother, daughter, friend, partner, professional. We identify with the roles we play, the things we manage, the people we love. Yet beneath all of that, what is constant?

When I look closely, I see that the "self" I refer to is not the role at all. I am a soul, the living consciousness expressing through this body. The body allows me to speak, act, and create. But the awareness behind those actions, the one who feels, chooses, and observes, is me, the soul.

True self-care begins when we care for that.

The Layers of the Self

We are layered beings. Body, emotion, mind, and soul are woven together, and each has its own language of care.

The body needs nourishment, movement, rest. It thrives on rhythm and attention. There's an entire industry built around physical care, and that care is real and necessary.

The emotions need acknowledgment. They ask to be felt, not fixed.

The mind and intellect need clarity, the dignity that comes from self-respect and accurate understanding.

And the soul, the essence behind all of it, lives in a reality of connection, silence, remembrance.

Take a moment to consider your relationship with each layer. How do you care for your body? Do you rest when it asks for rest? How do you care for your emotions? Do you allow them to speak, or do you silence them with activity? Do you offer your mind kindness or criticism?

These aren't questions for judgment. They're for distinction. You're learning to see where your energy actually goes, to notice the parts of yourself that have been waiting for attention.

Where We Give Away Our Power

Most of us live with our attention turned outward. We think the problem is what's happening around us, the circumstance, the person, the timing. But every time you focus outwardly for what only you can supply inwardly, you lose a little power.

This is the quiet exhaustion so many people feel. The fatigue of constantly trying to manage externals instead of caring for consciousness itself.

Think about someone you know who seems genuinely confident, someone who can stand their ground no matter what's happening around them. That quality comes from somewhere. It's self-respect rooted in something real, something internal.

For years, I never watched Western movies. They seemed pointless, just men staring at each other waiting to see who would move first. But I eventually realized what they're actually about: self-respect. Who has the most, who can remain most uninfluenced by the circumstances around them. The real drama is about inner stability.

The question for you is the same. Do you feel confident in different situations? Do you find yourself reacting, feeling powerless, getting emotionally upset? How do you feel about your relationship with your body?

These questions reveal where you've been focusing outward when you need to turn inward.

Meditation reverses that direction. It awakens the spiritual side of your existence, the part capable of observing rather than reacting. The moment you sit quietly and remember, "I am the soul using this mind," your energy begins to return. You start to stand inside your own life again.

The Two Secrets

There are two specific things that make self-care actually work, that move it from temporary relief to lasting transformation.

Attitude: The Energy Behind Everything

Attitude is the tone of energy behind every action. It's the invisible current others can feel even when you say nothing. You can be doing all the right things, exercising, working, caring for yourself, but if the attitude underneath is self-critical or careless, something in you remains unsatisfied.

Everyone can read your attitude. Just as you sense someone else's underlying energy, they sense yours. And most of us aren't responsible for it.

Consider this. You decide to take care of your body, to be healthy. But your underlying attitude is escape, so you eat to feel better in the moment and promise to deal with it later. The attitude might be procrastination, carelessness, resignation. The stated intention is care, but the attitude ensures care doesn't happen.

This shows up everywhere. You shower but your mind is elsewhere. You eat but you're annoyed. You rest but you're frustrated. What's your attitude when taking care of physical needs? What's your attitude toward your emotions? Do you get annoyed with yourself for feeling what you feel?

What attitude do you have toward yourself?

Imagine bringing an attitude of self-care into each small act. When you eat, let it be with gentleness toward your body. When you speak, let the tone itself be kind. Even when you shower or dress, notice whether your thoughts are with you or already racing elsewhere.

To care for yourself in truth is to infuse each moment with respect for your own existence. Not pride, but benevolence. The soul thrives in that atmosphere.

Start with one day. Bring an attitude of genuine care to one action you take for yourself. Notice what shifts.

The Right Medicine for Each Level

You cannot resolve a feeling with a thought. You have to resolve a feeling with a feeling.

When someone is hurting, logic rarely comforts. What heals is empathy, one feeling meeting another in understanding. The same is true within yourself. When your heart is heavy, analysis won't lighten it. What it needs is compassion.

Think about it. You feel upset. Someone says, "Well, you got what you deserved." Does that help? Of course not. When you're upset, you want someone to care. You want compassion, empathy. A feeling to meet your feeling.

The same principle applies to thoughts and actions. A thought helps a thought. An action helps an action.

We constantly use the wrong tool. We try to think our way out of feelings. We try to feel our way into different actions. Here's a common example. Someone says, "Yeah, I'll do that," then doesn't. You've probably done this. You say you'll change something but have no real intention of following through. The way to change that pattern isn't to feel bad about it or think about it differently. The way to change it is to actually do it. Action changes action.

With thoughts, we first have to know what we're thinking. This is where meditation becomes essential. You sit down and tell yourself, "I am a soul, my nature is peace," and suddenly your mind goes to the laundry or errands. You're seeing the thought pattern in action.

Getting angry won't change the thought. Feeling frustrated won't bring it back. You have to use another thought. Redirect: come back here. Guide the mind with the mind.

Every aspect of the self has its own medicine. If your actions are misaligned, act differently. If your thoughts are confused, observe them in meditation. If your feelings are raw, meet them with gentleness.

Healing comes when each level is cared for in its own language. This is the quiet art of spiritual self-care.

An Experiment in Awareness

For one day this week, pay attention to your attitude in ordinary moments. Notice how you approach your body, your emotions, your work. Are you moving through the day with care or with hurry?

Or try this: the next time a difficult feeling arises, pause. Instead of trying to reason it away, simply notice what kind of response would actually soothe it. Sometimes all that's needed is acknowledgment, a moment of inner warmth.

This is not effortful practice. It's merciful observation. You're learning to witness what's happening rather than to fix it.

The Emergence of Self-Respect

When you begin to live this way, self-care becomes less about improvement and more about integrity.

You start to sense an inner composure, a strength that doesn't need outer approval. This is self-respect in its spiritual form: the dignity of being aligned with what is true.

If you start being responsible for these levels, if you make even small changes, your self-respect begins to rise. You feel genuinely better. You become capable of decisions that actually serve you.

This doesn't happen overnight. Old attitudes and habits carry momentum and power. But with regular practice, things shift little by little. And they shift in a specific direction. Toward spirituality.

I am a soul. My nature is peace. My nature is loving, benevolent, pure, wise.

That's the attitude I want reflected in my thoughts, emotions, words, actions. One drop at a time, I move in that direction.

From that place, care for the body, emotions, and mind flows naturally. Nothing is forced. The soul's benevolent nature begins to shine through.

Real self-care is not about becoming someone new. It's about returning to yourself, the one who was peaceful all along. You transform by taking responsibility, by becoming aware of your patterns and shifting them. Eventually, you radiate a different quality, a spiritual vibration that comes from knowing who you actually are.

The result is that your authentic self shines through. You haven't constructed something new because the benevolent nature was always there. You just couldn't access it through all the unexamined patterns, mismatched responses, and attitudes you weren't responsible for.

Your true nature is already peaceful. Already loving. Already wise.

You're just learning how to stop blocking it.

Points for Contemplation

What is the attitude behind the way I care for myself?

Where do I act with good intention but a weary or doubtful energy?

When emotion arises, do I try to fix it with thinking, or do I allow it to be met with understanding?

Which part of me—body, emotion, or mind—is asking for care right now?

What would it feel like to move through my day with quiet self-respect, as the soul caring for its own creation?

Spiritual Daily Routine

YOU TAKE CARE OF everything. The laundry gets done. The bills get paid. The car receives its maintenance. Your body gets fed, clothed, cleaned. You manage relationships, work responsibilities, household tasks. An entire architecture of care surrounds you, built by you, sustained by you.

But when do you care for your mind?

Not your brain's physical health. Not productivity or time management. Your actual consciousness. The awareness that is reading these words right now. The one who feels, chooses, observes. When does that receive the same quality of attention you give to everything else?

The daily spiritual routine isn't about adding more tasks to an already full life. It's about meeting yourself before your patterns do, about establishing who you *actually are* before the day's momentum carries you into habitual ways of thinking and being.

The Architecture of Habit

Your mind operates on grooves worn deep by repetition. If you wake at 6:00 every morning, the thoughts and feelings that arrive at 6:00 are likely the same ones that arrived yesterday. The same worries surface. The same heaviness or hurry takes hold. The same internal conversation begins before you've even left the bed.

This is the mind's nature. It runs on pattern, on accumulated impressions that activate automatically. You don't choose these first thoughts any more than you choose your heartbeat. They simply begin, and you move through the day identified with them, believing they are you.

One of the first suggestions I give to new students is to set your alarm to wake up 30 minutes earlier than your normal wake up time. For Instance, if you typically wake up at 6:00, set your alarm for 5:30. This way the grooves of habit haven't activated yet. The mind hasn't fallen into its familiar channels. You have space to remember something else, to orient yourself differently before the day's momentum takes over.

This is why timing matters in spiritual practice. You're not trying to fight against established patterns. You're stepping in before they begin.

I once had a student who resisted morning meditation. She went through her entire routine in her mind: breakfast for her husband, the morning news, getting ready for work. "When would I meditate?" she asked. It genuinely hadn't occurred to her that she could wake before her routine started. The habits were so automatic she couldn't see past them.

That's what we're working with. This isn't laziness or resistance. Just deep grooves of repetition that feel like the only way things can be.

Meeting Yourself in Meditation: MORNING MEDITATION

The foundation of this routine is morning meditation. Not as luxury or reward, but as spiritual hygiene. You brush your teeth. You shower. These aren't optional if you want to stay healthy. The same is true for the mind.

Fifteen to twenty minutes, every morning. Before anything else.

Find a corner of your home where you do nothing but this. You don't need an elaborate setup. Just a chair, perhaps a small table with whatever supports your practice. This space becomes associated with one thing: remembering who you are.

Sit quietly. Close your eyes. And begin with the simplest truth: I am a soul. My original nature is peace.

You're not repeating words to convince yourself of something. You're turning attention inward, away from the body's sensations and the mind's noise, toward the consciousness observing both. The soul is the one aware. The body is the instrument. The mind is the collection of patterns. And you, the soul, the living consciousness, are distinct from all of it.

This distinction is what you're practicing.

Your mind will likely resist. Thoughts will flood in. The to-do list, yesterday's conversation, worries about later. This is normal. The mind has been running without observation for years. So, of course it continues.

But here's what matters: you sat down. You gave yourself those minutes. Even if the mind raced the entire time, you established that this matters, that you matter enough to receive this care. That's the victory.

If the mind feels too active, use guided meditations. Short practices that walk you through the remembrance, that keep bringing you back to "I am a soul, this is my nature." The guidance acts like training wheels until your own capacity strengthens.

The point isn't to achieve perfect silence. The point is to show up for yourself before the habits take over.

Feeding the Intellect: DAILY STUDY

After meditation, spend five to ten minutes with something that feeds your spiritual understanding. A few pages from scripture. A passage from this book or another that speaks to peace, forgiveness, patience. Whatever quality you're working to access more fully.

Read slowly. Not to accumulate information, but to let one idea land.

Then take that idea with you. Write it on a small piece of paper. Something simple: "My nature is benevolent." Or "I respond with patience." Put it in your pocket. This becomes your homework for the day.

Throughout your activities, you remember. You check in. When frustration rises, you touch the paper in your pocket and recall what you're actually practicing. This serves as a gentle redirection, reminding yourself of what you've chosen to cultivate.

The intellect needs this. It's been trained on worry, on problem-solving, on scanning for threats. Now you're retraining it toward your benevolent nature, giving it something true to work with instead of just reacting to circumstances.

Pausing the Momentum: TRAFFIC CONTROL

During the day, practice what might be called traffic control or mini- meditations. Two to three minutes where you stop completely.

If you're at your computer, turn away from the screen. Close your eyes. Sit still. Remind yourself: I am a soul. Everything around me is moving. The world is active. The body is active. Even the mind is active. But I, the consciousness, am still. My nature is peace.

This is so much more than a break from productivity. This is remembering what's actually happening. You're not the doing. You're the one aware of the doing. And that awareness can remain peaceful even as everything else moves.

These small pauses recharge something in you that pushing through never does. They interrupt the momentum of pattern. They create tiny spaces where you can distinguish yourself from the activity that pulls you forward.

Do this several times throughout the day.

Sharing What You've Cultivated: EVENING MEDITATION

In the evening, around 7:00, sit for meditation again. This time with a different quality.

Begin as always: I am a soul. My nature is peace. But now, as you feel that peace settling in you, share it. Extend it outward. Wish it for everyone.

Not for specific people. For all. All beings. All of nature. Everyone experiencing this moment on Earth. You're not solving their problems or changing their circumstances. You're simply holding the wish: may all feel peace. May all experience their own benevolent nature.

This is spiritual service. You're offering something real, the peace you've accessed through your own practice, and letting it ripple outward. You're participating in the world's healing not by doing more, but by being what you actually are and sharing that freely.

The meditation doesn't need to be long. Ten minutes. Fifteen if you're drawn to stay. The attitude matters more than duration. You're cultivating generosity of spirit, benevolence that extends beyond your immediate circle.

This practice shifts something in you. It moves you past the small concerns of "my life, my problems" into a larger sense of connection. The boundaries soften and you stop feeling so separate.

Learning Without Judgment: DAY REVIEW

Before sleep, review your day. Run it through your mind like watching a film.

How did the day unfold? Where did you remain peaceful? Where did old patterns activate? What did you notice about yourself?

This isn't about maintaining some perfect standard. You're investigating, getting curious, observing. Each day offers information about how the sanskars operate, where they're still running you, where you're beginning to distinguish yourself from them.

Maybe you reacted with impatience and only noticed hours later. That's fine. You noticed. That's the beginning. Maybe you caught yourself mid-reaction and could observe it happening. Even better. Maybe you saw the situation that usually triggers you and remained steady. Mark that quietly. Not with pride, but with recognition that something is shifting.

Whatever happened, make peace with it. Don't carry today's patterns into tomorrow's sleep. Let them go. You'll work with what needs attention when it surfaces again, which it will.

This nightly review builds your capacity to witness. You're training yourself to look at your own life with merciful clarity, to see what's there without turning away and without condemning what you find.

Why This Structure Works

This daily routine creates a container for transformation. Not through force or discipline, but through consistent care.

You begin by establishing your spiritual identity before the habitual mind activates. You feed your intellect with truth. You interrupt momentum throughout the day with stillness. You extend your peace outward in service. You observe yourself with mercy before rest.

Each element supports the others. The morning meditation makes the mini-meditations possible. The study gives you something to work with during the day. The evening meditation expands your self-care into world service. The nightly review helps you see what's actually shifting.

When I began this routine, I didn't implement everything at once. Some practices I gravitated toward immediately. Others took time. But I was consistent with morning meditation and study because something in me recognized these as essential.

After two weeks, anger had left. Not irritation or frustration, those remained. But anger itself, the explosive reactive quality that had run me for years, was simply gone. I didn't work directly on anger. I worked on remembering I am a soul, on establishing that truth first thing each morning before my patterns could claim me.

That's what this routine does. It doesn't fix you. It returns you to yourself. And from that place, patterns naturally lose their grip.

If you feel drawn to one aspect of the routine more than others, start there. But if you're going to choose just one practice, choose morning meditation. Everything else flows from that foundation. The capacity to witness, to distinguish yourself from your patterns, to access your benevolent nature—all of this develops through consistent meditation practice.

You're not building something new. You're clearing away what blocks your authentic nature from shining through. The benevolent self, the peaceful consciousness, the loving awareness—these are already what you are. You're learning to stop identifying with what covers them.

Points for Contemplation

Spiritual Daily Routine Summary
    1. **Morning Meditation** - sit for 15-20 minutes- starting

at least 30 minutes before your morning routine

2. **Study** - Read inspirational/spiritual material, and give yourself assignment for the day

3. **Traffic Control** - 3-5 minutes mini- meditation- remind myself of my spiritual nature

4. **Evening Meditation (Around 7pm)** - Focus on world service- share my peace, love, and good wishes with all souls and all of nature

5. **Day Review** - Review day before sleep- gain insights to keep moving forward in my progress

What parts of this daily routine are you attracted to?
What parts do you think would be a challenge to implement?

Merciful Self-Observation

M OST OF US SPEND years trying to change ourselves. We notice a pattern we don't like, maybe we're too reactive, too anxious, too critical, and we decide to fix it. We set intentions, push ourselves, and try harder when we "fail". Yet somehow the pattern persists, or worse, intensifies under the pressure of our effort.

There's a particular quality of attention that creates the conditions for real change. It's not about analyzing yourself better or trying harder. It's about learning to observe yourself with mercy.

This practice—merciful self-observation—is the foundation of spiritual transformation. Without it, you remain caught in the very patterns you're trying to escape. With it, everything begins to shift naturally.

What Mercy Actually Means

Before we can practice merciful self-observation, we need to understand what mercy is. The word has been so diluted that most people think it means being soft or permissive with themselves. That's not what I'm talking about.

Mercy has three distinct qualities.

First, there is love. You care. You have genuine good wishes for yourself. You're not indifferent to your own experience or dismissive of what you're going through. This caring is not conditional on your performance or behavior.

Second, there is understanding. You have wisdom about what's happening. You recognize context. You see where patterns came from and why they made sense at the time. This isn't excuse-making. It's clear-sighted recognition of cause and effect.

Third, there is detachment. You're not drowning in the emotion. You're not taking the pattern personally or letting it define you. You're present, caring, and clear, but not entangled. There's no transfer of emotional energy that pulls you down into suffering.

This is different from empathy, where you feel for someone. It's different from compassion, where you feel what they feel. In mercy, you understand what they're feeling because you have wisdom about it. You care deeply, but you're not affected in a way that diminishes your capacity to help.

When you bring this quality of attention to yourself, something remarkable happens. You stop abandoning yourself in the moments you most need support.

The Hidden Saboteur

Here's what most people don't realize: self-judgment hijacks spiritual progress.

You decide to work on yourself. You commit to meditation, to awareness, to change. Then you notice yourself falling into an old pattern—maybe you got angry, maybe you shut down, maybe you reacted in a way you promised yourself you wouldn't. And immediately, the judgment comes: "I'm doing it again. What's wrong with me? I should be past this by now."

This feels like spiritual effort. It feels like you're holding yourself accountable, pushing yourself toward growth. But look more carefully at what's actually happening.

When you judge yourself for having a pattern, you're generating the same harsh, critical energy that created many of your patterns in the first place. You're reinforcing the very consciousness you're trying to transform.

The judgment masquerades as something positive because you tell yourself you're trying to progress. But what it's actually stopping you from doing is feeling peaceful. It's stopping you from feeling love. It's stopping you from feeling hope.

I'll say it plainly: you cannot become peaceful through harsh internal criticism. You cannot become kind through judgment of yourself. You cannot access your benevolent nature while attacking yourself for not having accessed it yet. But there is hope.

Jesus said, "Love your neighbor as yourself." This is actually a law. However you relate to yourself is how you relate to others. If you're impatient with yourself, you're impatient with others. If you're judgmental of yourself, you're judgmental of others. The relationship is exact.

This means that when you transform the way you see and treat yourself, you automatically transform how you see and treat everyone else as well.

Observing Without Changing

Merciful self-observation means watching yourself—your thoughts, feelings, reactions, behaviors—with that quality of loving, understanding, detached attention. You're not trying to change anything. You're just watching, trying to understand.

This is harder than it sounds because we're so conditioned to immediately fix what we see.

Let me give you an example from my own practice. I grew up in an environment where everything was about scientific thinking, organizing, fixing, analyzing. I became what I call an Olympic-level organizer, an Olympic-level judger, an Olympic-level scientific analyzer. This was my training, my worldview, how I thought life worked.

Then I began spiritual practice and I was told to sit down and be still.

I couldn't do it. My mind was so active, so trained in constant motion. And I could have judged myself for that. I could have thought, "What's wrong with me? Why can't I do this simple thing?"

But merciful self-observation means recognizing: of course I can't be still right away. Look at where I came from. Look at what I've been trained to do. It takes time to change a worldview. It takes time to change deeply conditioned behaviors.

When I brought this understanding to my practice, when I watched myself with mercy instead of judgment, something began to shift. Not because I tried harder, but because I stopped fighting myself.

Two Dimensions of Self-Observation

You can observe yourself in two primary ways: your inner world and your outer behavior.

The inner world includes your thoughts, feelings, reactions, memories, everything happening beneath the surface. This is where most of the pattern lives. The story you're telling yourself about what's happening, the emotional charge you're carrying, the automatic associations your mind makes.

The outer dimension is your behavior: what you actually say and do in the world.

Both need attention. Sometimes the behavior is obvious but you don't see the inner pattern driving it. Other times you're very aware of what you're thinking and feeling but haven't noticed how it's showing up in your actions.

Merciful self-observation means watching both dimensions with that same quality of loving, understanding, detached attention. You're gathering information. You're building wisdom about how your particular mind works, how your patterns operate, where they came from.

Here's something crucial: bring the past, present, and future to bear on whatever you're observing.

If you see yourself reacting with anger, don't just observe what is happening in the moment. Look at the past. When did you learn to respond this way? What was happening in your life when this pattern formed? Look at the present. What's actually triggering you now? What need or fear is underneath the anger? Look at the future. If you keep responding this way, where will it lead?

This kind of observation builds understanding. And understanding, not judgment, creates the space for transformation.

What Happens When You Stop Abandoning Yourself

Think about what happens when someone you care about is struggling. If you have mercy for them, you don't abandon them. You stay present. You listen. You try to understand. You offer stability even when they can't feel stable themselves.

Most of us don't do this for ourselves. When we're struggling, when we're caught in a pattern, when we're suffering, we abandon ourselves through judgment. We withdraw our own caring presence right when we need it most.

There's research showing that babies don't survive without human contact. Even plants respond to attention. That caring presence, someone genuinely interested in your wellbeing, someone who sees you clearly without judgment, is essential for growth.

When you begin to give this to yourself through merciful self-observation, something fundamental shifts. You're no longer desperate for others to provide what only you can give yourself. You're no longer making others responsible for your sense of being seen, understood, or cared for.

You start to generate a different quality of internal energy. Not the harsh, driving energy of self-improvement. The gentle, steady energy that allows natural transformation.

The patterns don't necessarily disappear immediately. But they lose their power. You stop suffering from them in the same way. The triggers that once controlled you become phenomena you can watch with curiosity.

Points for Contemplation

How do I relate to myself? Am I kind to myself?

When I notice a pattern I don't like, what is my first response—judgment or curiosity?

What would I need if I could ask for one thing to help me feel better inside?

Can I choose one behavior or thought pattern this week and simply watch it with mercy, without trying to change it?

What does it feel like to imagine being the soul observing my patterns rather than being identified with them?

Try Merciful Self Observation three times today and write about it in your journal. How did it feel? What did you notice?

2

Transforming
Everyday Experiences

Why Can't I Rest?

I NTELLECTUALLY, REST MAKES SENSE. We understand that sleep matters, that breaks restore us, that constant motion eventually breaks the body down. Yet when the moment comes to actually stop, something inside us resists.

If we know rest is good for us, why do we find it so difficult?

The Pattern That Won't Stop

I grew up in the northeastern United States where the emphasis was clear: education, career, money, success. Everything centered on achievement. Hard work was the only path forward. Results were what mattered.

I built my entire life around action. Planning, thinking, doing, accomplishing. If someone suggested I "just be," I had no idea what they meant. My entire orientation toward existence was through doing something.

When you've lived this way long enough, rest doesn't just seem unnecessary. It seems wrong.

I knew people who could relax easily, who approached life with a laid-back attitude. And I judged them—harshly. Lazy.

Stupid. Useless. These were the actual words that ran through my mind when I encountered someone who wasn't as driven as I was.

Now consider what that judgment actually means. If I've associated rest with laziness and stupidity, with being *useless*, why would I ever allow myself to rest? I'd created a circular trap: I can't rest because rest means I'm worthless, so I keep moving, which prevents me from ever accessing rest.

This is the sanskar in action. Not just the pattern of constant motion, but the entire belief system underneath it that makes the pattern seem necessary, even virtuous.

What Lives Beneath the Judgment

The judgment I held toward relaxed people wasn't really about them. It was about my own inability to calm down.

I couldn't quiet my mind. I couldn't soothe my nervous system. And rather than acknowledge that incapacity, I made everyone who could do those things wrong. This is what arrogance often is: a cover for something we can't access in ourselves.

When I started practicing spirituality fourteen years ago, I had to face this directly. Even after I released the anger and resentment toward others, even after I stopped judging people as lazy, I still couldn't rest. The external judgment was gone, but the internal pattern remained.

This is an important distinction. You can change your attitude toward others and still carry the sanskar that prevents you from accessing what you need. The pattern runs deeper than conscious thought.

I am a soul. My nature is peace. But if I can't access that peace because I'm identified with constant motion, the truth of my nature remains theoretical. This is where practice becomes essential.

The Two Layers of Resistance

Rest has two aspects, and both require attention.

The physical exhaustion

Your body needs actual rest. Sleep, stillness, time away from stimulation. The nervous system needs to discharge. The muscles need to release. This is basic biology.

But you probably already know this. You know you should sleep more, take breaks, step away from screens. The information isn't the problem. The inability to act on it is.

The mental pattern

The deeper issue is the attitude you hold toward rest itself. What do you actually think about resting? Not what you believe you should think, but what you genuinely feel when the option to rest appears.

Do you see it as weakness? As wasted time? As something only unambitious people do?

These attitudes operate beneath conscious awareness most of the time. You might say you value rest while simultaneously resenting anyone who actually takes it. You might plan to relax on vacation while spending the entire week anxious about falling behind.

The attitude reveals the sanskar. And the sanskar is what you're learning to observe.

When Rest Becomes Available

Something shifted for me recently. I was talking with someone who mentioned they were "too lazy" to overthink and plan the way I do. They just let things unfold naturally.

For the first time, I didn't judge that response. I felt something closer to appreciation, even admiration. I recognized a capacity in them that I'd spent years condemning because I couldn't access it myself. This wasn't about becoming "lazy". It was about recognizing that constant mental activity isn't the only way to engage with life. That relaxation isn't the opposite of achievement. That rest itself is a form of intelligence.

When you can observe your patterns without identifying with them, they begin to lose their grip. I am the soul witnessing this sanskar of perpetual motion. The pattern still appears, but I'm no longer convinced it's who I am.

This is what makes rest possible: the recognition that you are not the pattern that prevents it.

The Practice of Merciful Observation

Most of us approach our patterns with the same driven energy that created them. We want to fix ourselves immediately, accomplish transformation, achieve peace. But that's still the sanskar operating. Instead, begin with simple observation using the points for contemplation below as a starting point.

The purpose isn't to catalog your failures. The purpose is to see clearly what's actually happening. You cannot shift a pattern you haven't fully recognized.

Once you've observed the pattern, once you've seen how it operates without judging yourself for having it, small changes become possible.

For me, eliminating Facebook was one small shift. I noticed I would scroll for hours, completely absorbed, and afterward feel depleted rather than rested. That wasn't actual rest. It was an attention trap disguised as relaxation.

I'm not suggesting you need to delete social media. I'm suggesting you notice what actually restores you and what merely distracts you from exhaustion.

Maybe you need more sleep. Maybe you need to stop working eighteen-hour days. Maybe you need to release the belief that constant productivity equals worth. Only you can discern what's true for your situation.

But the change must come from observation, not force. When you try to impose rest on yourself while still identified with the pattern that prevents it, you just create another form of doing. You're trying to achieve rest the way you achieve everything else.

Real rest emerges when you distinguish yourself from the sanskar. I am a soul. My nature is peace. The constant motion is just a pattern I've been carrying. It's not who I am.

Points for Contemplation

How do you actually feel about rest? Not how you think you should feel, but what arises when someone suggests you take a break.

Notice your thoughts when you see others resting. Do you judge them? Resent them? Feel superior to them?

Watch yourself throughout the day. Are you constantly active? Does your mind race even when your body is still? Do you feel good in this state, or do you feel exhausted, resentful, overwhelmed?

My Body My Friend

You came into this life with a body. From that first breath, the body has been with you. Through childhood, adolescence, every stage of development, the body has remained your constant companion.

Consider what the body provides. It gives you the ability to exist in time and space. To speak, touch, create. To give and receive. The body enables relationship, connection, every interaction you've had in the physical world.

The body also gave you specific circumstances. A nationality. A family. Gender, culture, perhaps education. All the conditions through which you experience this particular life came through the body.

This isn't gratitude practice. This is recognition of what's true.

The body has been your closest companion since birth. Most of us think about our bodies in terms of health, appearance, or function. We focus on what's working, what's changing, what needs improvement. But the deeper question is: who is relating to this body? Who is the one aware of these changes?

When I look closely, I see that I am not the body. I am the consciousness observing it, the soul using it to express in the world. This distinction isn't philosophical. It's the way things actually are.

When the Body Disappoints

Someone close to me was very sick once. During that illness, she said something that stayed with me: "I feel like my body is betraying me."

She had expected the body to remain healthy. When it didn't, she experienced betrayal.

Many of us carry some version of this feeling. The body ages. It gets sick. It changes in ways we didn't choose. Sometimes there are accidents, loss of function, chronic conditions. Sometimes the mind itself begins to fail through illness or age.

From a spiritual standpoint, these experiences are part of the body's nature. The body has its own timeline. It develops, matures, eventually declines. This is simply what bodies, as physical matter, do.

But we, the souls using these bodies, are not subject to that timeline.

This is where the distinction becomes essential. The body goes through stages. I, the soul, observe those stages. The body may struggle. I can remain peaceful while doing whatever needs to be done.

This isn't about positive thinking or acceptance in the psychological sense. It's about seeing clearly what's happening and who is experiencing it.

The Body's Natural Function

Right now, as you read this, your body is performing thousands of functions you're not consciously directing. Your heart beats. Your lungs breathe. Your senses process information. Systems regulate temperature, digest food, repair tissue.

The body maintains itself with remarkable intelligence.

Even when the body is sick or limited in some way, it's still functioning at whatever level it can. It's still serving as your vehicle for this life.

I've been experiencing bodily changes myself lately, transformations that come with a certain stage of life. As these changes happen, I notice my thoughts about them. I watch what the mind wants to make of these shifts.

The work is to separate my thinking from what's actually occurring. To distinguish my response from the body's process.

This distinction creates space. In that space, I can remain myself, the soul, even as the body transforms.

The Simple Truth Beneath Everything

We carry many ideas about the body. Fears about aging, illness, loss of capacity. Worries about appearance, performance, control. Information floods in constantly about what we should do, how we should care for ourselves, what might go wrong.

Beneath all of that sits a simple, essential relationship.

I am a soul. I am using this body to live this life. The body is my companion, my vehicle, my means of expression in this world.

This isn't a concept to understand. It's a reality to experience.

51

When you sit in meditation each morning and remember "I am a soul, my nature is peace," you're not creating something new. You're returning to what's true. The body continues its processes. Thoughts come and go. But you remain. The consciousness observing it all.

From that place of clarity, everything shifts. The body's changes become phenomena you can witness without losing yourself. You remain peaceful while doing whatever the situation requires.

This is spiritual self-respect. Not pride in the body's abilities or appearance. But recognition of your own eternal nature, distinct from the temporary vehicle you're using.

Your body is not betraying you when it changes. It's doing what bodies do. You are not your body. You're the one aware of it, caring for it, living through it.

Points for Contemplation

When the body changes or struggles, do I feel betrayed? Or can I observe the change while remaining peaceful?

Can I distinguish between what the body is experiencing and what I, the soul, am experiencing?

What would shift if I truly recognized the body as my faithful companion rather than as my identity?

In meditation today, can I simply observe the body functioning and recognize myself as the consciousness aware of it?

This week, observe your relationship with your body with mercy. Notice when you identify as the body versus when you observe as the soul. Don't judge what you see. Just watch with curiosity and clarity.

Money + Common Sense

T HE WORLD TELLS US money is something external, a resource we manage, earn, or struggle with. We see it as separate from our spiritual life, something practical that has little to do with peace or consciousness. I invite you to expand this understanding by considering what your relationship with money reveals about your relationship with yourself.

Money isn't just currency. It's energy. It represents your life value, your time, your capacity to create and contribute. The way it flows through your life, the way you hold it or avoid it, the respect you show it or the chaos you allow around it—all of this mirrors something essential about your inner state.

When you're drowning in debt, peace becomes nearly impossible. When you're managing responsibly but without care for yourself, you're surviving but not thriving. And when you're able to give freely, to direct financial energy toward something meaningful, you're expressing your benevolent nature.

This chapter is about seeing money as spiritual practice, recognizing where you stand, and understanding what shift is actually possible.

The Truth About Debt

I remember the exact moment I stepped into debt. I was eighteen, standing in a store, wanting something I couldn't afford. The thought came: I should wait until I have the money. Then immediately after: I can just charge it.

That second thought felt like a door opening. It seemed harmless, convenient even. But what I didn't see was that I was crossing a line, moving from living within my means to living in a fantasy where future money would somehow solve present desire.

That moment led to $36,000 in debt. Credit cards, all of it unsecured, all of it accumulating while I told myself I'd deal with it later. The weight of it was crushing. Not just the bills, but what it did to my sense of self. I couldn't feel good about myself while owing that much. I couldn't feel independent. I couldn't feel at peace.

Debt isn't just a financial problem. It's a spiritual one. When you owe, you contract. Your self-respect diminishes. You lose access to your own benevolent nature because you're constantly in a state of deficit, not just financially but internally.

If you're in debt right now, you know this feeling. The anxiety, the shame, the way it colors everything else. This is where healing must begin.

The Three Levels

Think of your relationship with money as existing on three levels simultaneously. You're not progressing through them in sequence. You're working with all three at once, but each requires something different from you.

The first level is debt. If you're here, the priority is clear: get out. This isn't about judgment. It's about recognizing that debt blocks your access to peace. You cannot build self-respect on a foundation of owing.

The path out requires discipline and often help. I had a friend who understood money in ways I didn't. I told her I'd do whatever she said. She put me on cash-only for six months. Every purchase required a receipt. No credit cards, no debit cards, just cash and accountability.

It worked because it made every transaction conscious. I couldn't float through spending. I had to see the money leave my hand. That simple practice rewired something in me.

If you're in significant debt, consider getting help. A trusted friend, a debt consolidation service, something that creates structure and accountability. Then make a decision: once you're out, you never go back. I've lived without carrying credit card debt for over twenty years. That line, once I crossed back over it, I never crossed again.

The second level is responsible management. This is where most people live. You're not drowning, but you're juggling. Bills, expenses, trying to provide for others while taking care of yourself. The question here isn't just about making ends meet. It's about the quality of your choices.

Are you operating within your means? Are you taking care of yourself, not just surviving but actually nourishing your body, your life, your environment? Are you fulfilling your responsibilities to others with the same care?

This level requires discernment. Common sense, yes, but also an awareness of what actually matters. You're learning to direct energy wisely, to make decisions that honor both your needs and your values.

The third level is service. This is where money becomes spiritual practice in its fullest form. You have enough. Your needs are met. Now the question becomes: where can this energy serve something beyond my immediate life?

My father plays poker a couple times a week. When he wins, he sends half to St. Jude Children's Hospital. He loves that. Not because it makes him look good, but because he genuinely feels that the money is doing something meaningful. He's directing the energy toward healing.

This is what service with money looks like. You find something you believe in, something genuinely helping others, and you put your financial energy there. Not out of obligation or guilt, and definitely not to receive accolades, but because you recognize that giving is the highest use of what you have.

I contribute to the Brahma Kumaris because I know they're teaching meditation and spiritual knowledge freely around the world. I've seen the impact. I trust where the energy goes. That matters. Choose your service wisely. Research. Make sure the money actually reaches what you care about.

Money as Self-Respect

Here's what I've learned: you cannot feel genuine self-respect while lying to yourself about money.

If you're in debt and pretending you're not, if you're overspending and calling it self-care, if you're avoiding looking at your actual financial situation, something inside you knows the truth. And that knowing erodes your foundation.

Self-respect, the spiritual kind, comes from integrity. From alignment between what you know is true and how you're actually living.

When you face your debt honestly, when you manage your money with care and consciousness, when you give with genuine intention, something shifts. You start to trust your own judgment. You feel capable. You feel dignified.

This doesn't require accumulating wealth. It's about the energy you bring to money. Someone with very little can have tremendous self-respect around finances if they're living with integrity, making conscious choices, directing their limited resources wisely and with care.

Someone with abundance can have almost no self-respect if they're careless, impulsive, using money to avoid feeling what they feel or to prove something they don't actually believe about themselves.

The amount isn't the point. The consciousness is.

The Return to Your Benevolent Nature

When you bring consciousness to money, when you clear debt, manage responsibly, and give with intention, you're clearing away what's been blocking your benevolent nature.

The soul's nature is generous, peaceful, dignified. But when you're trapped in financial chaos or carelessness, you can't access that. The sanskars around money—fear, greed, shame, avoidance—create a barrier.

As you work with these three levels, as you bring honesty and care to your financial life, those sanskars lose their grip. You start to experience yourself as capable, as trustworthy, as someone who can direct energy wisely.

This is spiritual self-respect, earned not through achievement, but revealed through integrity.

Points for Contemplation

First, be honest. Do you have debt? If so, how does it feel inside your body when you think about it? Notice that. Don't judge it. Just see it clearly.

Second, look at your daily financial choices. Are you operating within your means? Are you taking care of yourself? Are you meeting your responsibilities? Where might you need to make an adjustment?

Third, consider service. Where, if anywhere, are you directing financial energy beyond your immediate needs? Is there something you genuinely care about that could benefit from your contribution?

Reducing Relationship Stimuli

E VERY INTERACTION CARRIES AN energetic current. You can feel it when someone enters a room, when a conversation begins, when your phone lights up with a message. There's a flow that moves between people, an exchange that happens whether we acknowledge it or not.

This isn't abstract. You know the feeling of being drained after certain conversations. You know the relief when someone finally leaves. You also know the warmth of genuine connection, when the exchange feels nourishing rather than depleting.

The question is: when do you get to feel what's actually happening inside you, without that constant current running through your awareness?

I grew up in a culture of constant sharing. Everything was talked about, processed aloud, shared immediately. My mother and I were close. My female friends and I told each other everything. There was always someone to call, always someone who wanted to know what I was thinking. It felt like love, like connection, like how relationships were supposed to work.

But I never learned to simply sit with my own experience. I never developed the capacity to observe what I felt without immediately turning it into a conversation and seeking input from friends and family. My identity was woven through all those connections. I existed in the exchange.

Many people live this way. Especially women, though men have their own versions. The phone is always within reach. The sharing never stops. Every thought becomes a text, every experience a story to tell.

And then one day you notice: you're exhausted. You don't know what you actually think or feel because you've never given yourself space to find out.

Where the Energy Goes

Years ago, I had a student in her eighties. We were discussing how relationships can drain us, how we can set up patterns where we're always available, always taking care of others, always in the flow of someone else's need.

I asked her how many people she had in her life like that. People she was fully invested in, picking up the phone any time, doing things for them, giving her all.

She said eight.

Eight people. Can you imagine having eight people in your life that you're completely available to, that you're energetically merged with, that pull on your attention and care at all hours? This isn't necessarily negative. These might be good relationships, loving relationships. But if you're always in the exchange, always responding, always available, when do you replenish? When does your consciousness get to rest and observe itself?

The soul can't witness its own patterns when it's constantly engaged in external connection. You remain identified with the sanskar of caretaking, of people-pleasing, of deriving worth from being needed. You can't see the pattern because you're living inside it.

The First Boundary

I remember the moment I decided to create space. It wasn't a dramatic decision. I simply told myself: I won't answer the phone after eight in the evening.

One boundary. That's all it was.

But a tension I didn't know I carried relaxed. I had given myself permission to not be available, to let the current stop flowing for a few hours. It felt like coming up for air.

Later, I made another boundary at work. I joked with my team: don't talk to me before ten in the morning. It was said lightly, but it was also real. I need that morning time to gather my energy, to orient myself, to be present without immediately engaging in conversation and decision-making and the full energetic exchange of work.

These aren't rules. They're statements of self-knowledge. This is how I function well. This is what I need to remain conscious and present. This is how I take care of the soul using this body and mind.

When you create even one boundary, you're telling yourself something important: I matter. My inner experience matters. My recovery matters.

A boundary isn't against anyone. It's simply you saying: I know who I am, I know what I need, and I'm telling you.

Most people respect this. They feel relieved, actually, because now they know where they stand. They know how to treat you. They're not guessing or trying to read signals. You've given them clarity, and that clarity allows them to win with you.

You're setting them up to succeed in the relationship because you've been honest about what you need.

The Return to Relationship

Here's what happens when you reduce the constant stimuli.

You come back to interactions feeling stronger. You're not as reactive, not as vulnerable, not as desperate for validation or connection. You can be present without losing yourself in the exchange.

The relationships don't suffer. They improve. Because now you're showing up from inner fullness rather than need.

I notice this in my work. When I honor my morning boundary, when I give myself that time, I'm better with people later. I'm clearer, more patient, more genuinely present. When I violate the boundary, when I let myself be pulled into full engagement too early, I feel scattered all day. The same is true with personal relationships. When I take time for myself, when I meditate daily and create space for my own inner experience, I return to my relationships with actual love rather than obligation. I can listen without the underlying resentment that comes from being drained. I can give without feeling depleted.

Some relationships are toxic. Some need to end or be radically restructured. That's a different conversation. But most relationships simply need boundaries. They need you to know yourself well enough to say: this is how much connection serves me. This is when I need to step back and recover.

When you begin living with boundaries, something emerges that was always there but couldn't be accessed: your benevolent nature.

The soul's capacity for genuine love, real compassion, actual kindness. Not the performance of these things, not the exhausting effort to be good and caring and always present. But the natural expression of a consciousness that knows itself.

That benevolence can only flow naturally when I'm not depleted, not merged, not lost in constant exchange. When I know myself clearly enough to say: this is what I need. This is who I am. From that place, relationship becomes something entirely different. Not a place to lose yourself, but a place to express what you already are.

Points for Contemplation

This week, notice your patterns of availability. Don't try to change anything yet. Just observe.

How quickly do you respond to messages? Do you feel anxiety if you don't answer immediately? Do you pick up the phone even when you don't want to?

Notice the energetic current in your relationships. Which ones feel nourishing? Which ones leave you depleted? Not because the people are bad, but because the pattern of exchange is unbalanced.

Then consider: what would one boundary look like? Not eight boundaries. Not a complete restructuring of your life. Just one small declaration of self-knowledge. One time of day when you're not available. One type of conversation you don't engage in. One way you protect your morning or evening or weekend time.

Pros and Cons of Media

W E HOLD THE WHOLE world in our hands. Information, connection, entertainment, work—all of it accessible in an instant. This convenience has transformed how we live. It has removed barriers, leveled access, and made communication immediate. A teenager in a small town has the same information available as a CEO of a corporation in a major city. That's remarkable.

But the convenience comes at a cost. When everything is instantly available, when there are no natural pauses built into our days, we need to look honestly at what we're actually reaching for. Are we reaching for information, or are we reaching away from silence? Are we connecting with others, or disconnecting from ourselves?

What Technology Actually Reveals

Technology itself is neutral. The phone doesn't create the problem. It reveals patterns that were already there—patterns of avoidance, distraction, dependency. It shows us where we give our attention unconsciously, where we lose sovereignty over our own awareness.

When I pick up my phone without deciding to, when I scroll without purpose, when I reach for the screen because I'm uncomfortable with what I'm feeling, that's not the technology's fault. That's a sanskar appearing. The phone simply makes it visible.

This is why judging technology misses the point. The spiritual work isn't to reject screens or fear what they're doing to us. The work is to become conscious of how we use them, to distinguish between the soul making a choice and old patterns running automatically.

You are a soul. You use this body, this mind, these tools. But somewhere along the way, many of us forgot that distinction. We became what we use instead of remaining the one who uses.

The Progression of Control

There's a framework that helps clarify where we stand with anything that has the potential to pull us away from conscious living. It moves through four stages: use, abuse, dependency, addiction.

Most frameworks like this are applied to substances, but they work equally well for screens, for relationships, for any pattern where we might lose our center.

Use is straightforward. I'm using the tool for what it's designed to do. I need directions, I look them up. I want to call someone, I make the call. The soul is present, making choices aligned with priorities. There's nothing problematic about use.

Abuse appears when attraction to the screen begins to override other priorities. A teenager scrolls instead of doing homework. Adults sit at dinner looking at phones instead of speaking to each other. The pull toward the screen becomes stronger than the pull toward presence, toward responsibility, toward relationship.

Notice what's underneath abuse: something else has become more important than what actually matters. The priorities—connection, purpose, self-care, growth—get displaced. Not because the technology is inherently harmful, but because I'm using it to avoid what I don't want to face.

Dependency is subtler. This is where I've begun to need the screen to feel normal. I'm using it to manage emotions, to fill empty moments, to soothe anxiety or boredom. The phone becomes mood-altering. I reach for it automatically when I feel uncomfortable. I've created a pattern where my emotional state depends on the distraction it provides.

Most of us have some level of dependency. We've normalized it. But normalization doesn't mean it's conscious. It just means we've stopped noticing.

Addiction is when I've convinced myself I literally cannot live without it. The thought of being without the phone creates panic. I check it constantly, even when there's no reason to. The dependency has become so complete that I've lost the awareness that I could choose differently.

Here's what matters spiritually: at each stage, I'm moving further from soul consciousness and deeper into identification with the pattern. Use keeps me sovereign. Abuse begins the loss of control. Dependency makes me believe the external thing is necessary for my internal state. Addiction convinces me I have no choice at all.

The soul always has a choice. But when I'm identified with the sanskar, I forget that.

The Silence That Teaches

A few years ago, my husband and I went to India for a five day silence retreat. There were sixty other people, all serious meditators from around the world. The first day was preparation. Then four days of complete silence. No phones, no laptops, no screens of any kind.

What surprised me most was that it didn't bother me. I thought it would. I expected to feel the pull, the discomfort of separation. But I didn't.

Part of the reason was preparation. I knew it was coming. I had time to adjust mentally. But the larger reason was the attitude surrounding the practice. There was no judgment about technology, no righteousness about being screen-free. The teachers respected what technology offers. They simply said: now we're putting it aside for a while so we can pay attention to ourselves.

That respect made all the difference.

When we prove to ourselves that we can live without something, we stop being controlled by it. The dependency loosens. We remember: I am the soul. I don't need this external thing to be at peace. My nature is peace.

Most people never test this. They stay in the dependency without realizing it could be otherwise. A periodic fast—a day, a weekend, even a few hours in the evening—reminds you what's true. You can live without it. And in that space where the screen isn't filling every moment, you start to notice what it was covering.

Sometimes it's restlessness. Sometimes it's loneliness. Sometimes it's just the discomfort of being with yourself without distraction.

That's the real gift of silence. Not the absence of the phone, but the presence of what the phone was helping you avoid.

Service and Self-Care as Transformation

There's a way to use technology that keeps you in the realm of conscious choice rather than unconscious pattern. It requires honesty about what you're actually doing with it.

Look at your phone right now. What apps do you have? What content do you consume? Is any of it elevating your consciousness? Is any of it contributing to your growth, your service, your spiritual practice?

Or is most of it distraction? Entertainment that numbs rather than nourishes? Content that triggers comparison, gossip, negativity?

I'm not saying entertainment is wrong. I'm asking: is what you're consuming in alignment with your personal and spiritual aims? Does it match the person you wish to be?

When you use screens for service—to share something helpful, to connect meaningfully, to learn something that expands your awareness—you're using them as the soul would use them. The energy is different. You're contributing rather than consuming, creating rather than escaping.

When you use them for self-care—to meditate, to listen to uplifting content, to connect with wisdom—you're nourishing yourself rather than numbing yourself.

The shift from abuse to use often comes from this simple adjustment: purpose. When I know why I'm picking up the phone, when I'm using it for something aligned with my values, I remain conscious. When I'm picking it up to avoid feeling something, I've slipped back into pattern.

This doesn't require perfection. It requires awareness. The soul observing the sanskar: I see what I'm reaching for. I see why. And I can choose differently.

Mastery Without Fear

We don't need to be afraid of technology. We don't need to reject it or condemn it. What we need is to master our relationship with it.

Mastery means the soul remains sovereign. I use the tool. The tool doesn't use me.

This comes from honest self-observation. Where do I lose control? When do I reach for the screen unconsciously? What am I using it to avoid?

These questions aren't meant to produce shame. They're meant to produce clarity. When you see the pattern clearly, when you distinguish yourself from it, it loses power.

I mentioned earlier that I have some dependency. I use screens to manage emotions sometimes. That's the truth. But because I can see it, because I'm not identified with it, I can work with it. I can choose to take breaks. I can fast from screens in the evenings. I can audit my apps and remove what doesn't serve me.

The work is ongoing. Patterns have momentum. But each time I choose consciousness over automaticity, I strengthen my spiritual identity. I am a soul. I am not controlled by external things. My peace comes from within.

That's the real transformation technology can facilitate. Not through what it gives us, but through what it reveals about where we still need to grow.

True mastery of media isn't about rules or restrictions. It's about returning to yourself.

You are a soul. Your nature is peace, love, wisdom. You don't need anything external to access that nature. But when you're constantly distracted, constantly reaching outward, you forget what's already present within.

Technology can be a tool for remembering or a tool for forgetting. The choice is always yours.

Points for Contemplation

Where do I fall on the continuum of use, abuse, dependency, and addiction with screens?

What am I using technology to avoid feeling or facing?

If I were to fast from screens for one day, what would arise in that space?

Do my apps and digital habits reflect who I am becoming spiritually?

When I pick up my phone, what is my attitude? Am I reaching for something purposeful or reaching away from discomfort?

How could I transform one screen habit into an act of service or self-care?

Instant Emotional Control

EMOTIONAL OVERWHELM FEELS LIKE something that happens *to* us, a force we can't control once it takes hold. The racing thoughts arrive, the worry spirals, and we're swept into it like a current pulling us under. But what happens when we ask *who* is noticing that you're overwhelmed?

This distinction matters. Because if something in you can recognize "I'm overwhelmed," then not all of you is overwhelmed. There's a witness. There's a part that sees.

This chapter offers a technique that makes that witness immediately accessible, even in the middle of emotional chaos. It's simple enough to use in real time, yet profound enough to shift your relationship with your own mind.

When the Mind Convinces You of Crisis

You know this experience. The circumstances around you aren't the way you want them to be. Maybe it's uncertainty about money, a problem with your vehicle, a situation at work where you don't have enough information. Nothing catastrophic is actually happening. No one is in physical danger.

But internally, you feel stimulated, afraid, unable to stop thinking about it.

The thoughts come fast. What if this happens? What if I can't handle it? What should I do? The questions multiply, each one generating more anxiety. Your body feels it too, that elevated nervous energy, the subtle or not-so-subtle sensation of fight or flight.

This is what makes emotional overwhelm so convincing. It feels like crisis even when logic says otherwise. The fearful energy hijacks clear thinking. You can't make decisions from that place. You can't see options. The mind has taken you somewhere, pulled you into an experience that feels urgent and real.

But here's what's actually true: when you're in that state, there's still a part of you that isn't swept away. The part that knows you're upset. The part that can think, "I need to calm down." That part is always there, always observing, always capable of choice.

The technique I'm about to share helps you access that part immediately.

Give It a Percentage

When you notice yourself in emotional overwhelm, racing thoughts, worry that won't stop, pause and ask yourself one question: What percentage of me is upset right now, and what percentage is calm and logical?

Just assign numbers. Don't overthink it. The first response that comes is usually accurate.

A student of mine called once, deeply worried about her vehicle. She had animals she needed to transport, circumstances weren't lining up, and her mind was spinning with what-ifs. She couldn't stop thinking about it. Nothing was actually broken, but inside she felt completely overwhelmed.

I asked her the question. She said immediately: "Ninety-nine percent upset. One percent calm."

That one percent is everything.

Because the moment you assign a percentage, you're doing something radical. You're using your intellect to evaluate your own mind. You're distinguishing yourself from the experience. The very act of measuring creates distance.

Math has no emotion. It's pure logic. When you say "ninety-nine percent," you're stepping outside the overwhelm long enough to observe it.

Why the Percentage Works

The percentage technique works because it activates what's already true: you are not your emotions. You are the consciousness aware of them.

Think about it. If one percent of you is calm, that means calm is present. It's not something you have to create or manufacture. It's already there, just drowned out by the noise of the ninety-nine percent.

Now here's the key: you don't try to change the ninety-nine percent. You don't fight it or try to talk yourself out of being upset. You simply focus on the one percent.

I told my student: concentrate on that one percent. Dive into it. Let the ninety-nine percent be there, but put your attention fully on the part of you that's still calm, still capable of clear thinking, still grounded in reality.

She did. And within minutes, the overwhelm began to lose its grip. The circumstances hadn't changed, but she stopped identifying with the emotional reaction. She remembered: I am not this fear. I am the one observing it.

This is spiritual practice in action. You're training yourself to witness rather than become.

The Part That Sees

Every emotion, every racing thought, every fear-based reaction happens in the mind. But there's always something watching it happen. Even in the most intense overwhelm, there's a part of you that registers "I'm overwhelmed."

That part is you. The soul. The consciousness that uses the mind but is not the mind itself. In meditation, we practice this distinction directly. We sit and observe thoughts arising. We notice feelings in the body. We recognize patterns. And through that observation, we begin to experience ourselves as separate from what we're observing.

The percentage technique brings that meditative awareness into daily life. It's a way of saying: even here, even in the middle of this emotional storm, I can remember who I am.

You might give yourself ninety-nine and one. Or eighty and twenty. The specific numbers don't matter. What matters is the act of evaluation itself. The moment you assess, you're no longer drowning. You're standing on shore watching the water. And from that place, you can think clearly. You can make decisions. You can remember that nothing is actually wrong right now, that you're capable of handling whatever comes.

This isn't about positive thinking or forcing yourself to feel better. It's about truth. The truth is that you are a soul, and your nature is peace. That peaceful nature doesn't disappear when emotions rise. It just gets obscured. The percentage technique clears the obstruction.

From Identification to Mastery

Every time you use this technique, you're choosing soul consciousness over mind consciousness. You're choosing to witness rather than become.

This is the work of this book. You've learned that you are a soul. Now you're learning to live from that understanding, to access it in real time, to let it guide you even when the mind is loud.

The percentage technique is one tool among many. But it's powerful because it's immediate. You don't need perfect circumstances. You don't need to wait until you're calm. You can use it right in the middle of chaos.

And each time you do, you strengthen the muscle of self-mastery. You prove to yourself that you are not at the mercy of your emotions. You have the capacity to observe, to distinguish, to choose.

Points for Contemplation

When was the last time I felt emotionally overwhelmed? What was the experience like? If I had paused in that moment and asked "what percentage of me is upset?" what would the answer have been?

Can I identify the part of me that observes my emotions, even when they're intense?

What does it feel like to consider that I am not my racing thoughts or fears, but the consciousness aware of them?

What percentage of me right now, in this moment, is calm and present?

Deep Cleanse My Life

W E LIVE IN A culture of accumulation. More possessions, more commitments, more options, more connections. The assumption is that having more gives us more freedom, more security, more happiness. But living surrounded by excess does something to consciousness itself. It changes how the mind functions, how peace becomes available, how much energy remains for what actually matters.

Think of walking into a hotel room. Everything is in place. The floor is clean, the linens fresh, nothing unnecessary cluttering the space. There's something quietly supportive about that orderliness, a sense of ease you can feel immediately. The environment itself invites rest.

Now consider your own surroundings. Your home, your schedule, your relationships. How many things are you carrying that you don't actually need? How much of your attention goes to managing what could simply be released?

Recognize that everything you keep—every object, every commitment, every unresolved relationship—requires your care. And when you're caring for too much, you lose access to the simplicity that allows the soul to breathe.

What We Carry Without Noticing

Physical surroundings impact consciousness more than we realize. Everyone has a threshold for this, a point at which clutter or excess begins to weigh on the mind.

Imagine a room that could comfortably hold forty people. Put five people in that space and notice how it feels—open, breathing, easy. Now put a hundred people in the same room. The walls haven't changed, but everything feels different. Now it is crowded, overwhelming, and difficult to move.

Your life works the same way. When you're surrounded by too much, too many possessions, too many obligations, too many unexamined patterns, your consciousness feels crowded. The mind can't settle. Peace becomes something you have to reach for rather than something naturally present.

Whatever you have, you must care for. From a spiritual perspective, anything in excess is impacting your mind whether you're aware of it or not.

This extends beyond physical surroundings. Relationships can carry excess too. For years, I had friendships with no boundaries. When I had a friend, I would be on the phone with them all hours, constantly available, giving all my attention without taking care of myself.

That's too much. Not because caring is wrong, but because overextension obscures your capacity to care from a clear place.

The first step in deep cleansing is simple observation. Look at your life with mercy and understanding. Not to blame yourself for letting things get out of control, but to see honestly: where do I feel crowded? Where is there too much? Which areas feel uncomfortable or exhausting?

This requires courage because you're going against patterns that may have been there for years. But it also requires gentleness. You're not attacking yourself. You're investigating what's true.

Removing What Blocks Contentment

Simplification isn't about deprivation. It's about removing what stands between you and your natural state of contentment.

Start small. If the thought of organizing your life feels overwhelming, begin with something manageable. One drawer. One commitment. One boundary you can hold for a week.

I remember working with someone who couldn't imagine tackling the clutter in her home. Even thinking about it created resistance. So we started with her dresser drawers. Just keeping her clothing organized and put away. It sounds insignificant, but when you do something like that—when you create order in one small area and maintain it—self-respect begins to rise. You start to feel capable.

This is the quiet art of transformation: taking responsibility in small ways until you recognize your own strength.

From Outer Order to Inner Peace

Deep cleansing applies to every area of life. Consider where you might begin.

Home environment: Look around with honest eyes. Are you happy with the level of cleanliness and order? If ten represents complete satisfaction, where would you place each room? Your bedroom. Your closet. Your kitchen. Not to judge, but to see.

Some people thrive with minimal possessions. Others need more to feel comfortable. There's no single standard. The question is whether your environment matches your values and supports your peace.

I've found that having very little in my home helps my mind settle. My closet is nearly empty. Not because I'm ascetic, but because I feel better this way. I have what I need without carrying what I don't.

If physical organization overwhelms you, talk to someone who's good at it. Spend time in a friend's uncluttered home. Notice how it feels. Let that feeling become a reference point.

Relationships: Where do you overextend? Where are there no boundaries? It's possible to care deeply for people while maintaining clarity about what you can actually give. You can fulfill responsibilities without becoming overwhelmed.

One thing that helped me was spending more time alone. Not isolation, but intentional solitude. Time to know myself independently of others' needs and expectations. In relationships, I had become overly pleasing, trying to get people to like me even though in other areas of life I was quite accomplished. The pattern didn't match the rest of my experience, but I couldn't see it clearly until I gave myself space.

When you spend time in your own company, you build independent self-respect. You discover what you actually think and feel rather than what you've learned to perform.

Family: These relationships often come with expectations formed long ago. It's okay to examine what you feel comfortable with and adjust accordingly. You can still fulfill your responsibilities while caring for yourself.

My father is retired. My mother passed away three years ago. I'm the main person helping my dad, and when he was sick recently, I made myself available. But generally I'm still having my life. It doesn't feel overwhelming because I've learned to focus on what's essential to the relationship while maintaining my own care.

There's a way to balance self-care with caring for others. It requires honesty about your capacity and willingness to set boundaries that protect your peace.

Work and commitments: Look at where you've said yes automatically. Where do you feel overextended? Where could you simplify without abandoning responsibility?

Every little movement toward simplification brings relief. You begin to see that you don't need as much as you thought. What you need is clarity about what matters and the courage to release what doesn't.

What Reveals Itself When Excess Falls Away

When you begin simplifying your life, two things happen.

First, your mind becomes quiet and uncluttered. You have less to think about, less to manage, less pulling at your attention. In that quiet, contentment emerges. Not the contentment of having everything you want, but the contentment of recognizing you have what you need.

Contentment means you're not reaching for something else. You're not waiting for circumstances to change before you can feel at peace. Everything is enough, exactly as it is.

Second, self-respect naturally arises. When your home reflects your values, when your relationships have healthy boundaries, when your commitments match your capacity—you feel proud of yourself. Not ego-proud, but spiritually dignified. You recognize your own benevolent capacity to create a life that supports your true nature.

Deep cleansing your life is not self-improvement. You're not becoming someone better. You're removing what blocks access to your benevolent nature, which was always there.

The peace you're looking for isn't created by organization or simplification. It's revealed by it. When you stop carrying what you don't need—physically, relationally, mentally—the soul's natural simplicity shines through.

Points for Contemplation

Which areas of my life feel crowded or excessive right now?

If contentment means having enough, what would "enough" actually look like in my home, my schedule, my commitments?

What one small change could I make this week that would support my sense of order and peace?

When I imagine living with less—fewer possessions, fewer obligations, fewer unexamined patterns—what feeling arises?

How does the simplicity of my outer life support the clarity of my meditation practice?

Where have I been carrying what I don't need, and what would it feel like to set it down?

Peace at Work

M ODERN AMERICANS SPEND MORE waking hours at work than anywhere else. We invest years of training, decades of effort, entire identities in what we do professionally. Yet work is often where we feel most powerless, most reactive, most unlike the person we want to be.

We tell ourselves the problem is external. The boss who doesn't recognize us. The colleagues who don't understand. The position we deserved but didn't get. The compensation that doesn't match our worth. We believe that if those circumstances would just change, we'd finally feel at peace.

Yet the circumstances aren't actually the problem. The problem is what we've made them mean about us.

The Agreement We Forget

Work is an agreement. You provide a service, skill, or labor. Someone compensates you with money and benefits. That's the actual relationship.

This may sound cold, but it's clarifying. When you strip away everything you've layered onto work—your identity, your self-worth, your need for validation—what remains is a transaction. A mutually beneficial exchange.

The suffering at work doesn't come from the work itself. It comes from forgetting this basic truth and making work mean something it was never designed to mean.

You are a soul. Your nature is peace, wisdom, benevolence. That doesn't come from a job title, a promotion, or anyone's recognition. It's what you are beneath all the accumulated patterns and reactions.

When you make work more than an agreement, when you attach your sense of self to it, you create the conditions for suffering. Because now every disappointment feels personal. Every setback feels like defeat. Every moment of not getting what you think you deserve feels like evidence that something is fundamentally wrong with you.

It isn't.

Where the Pain Actually Lives

There are common places where work triggers suffering. The work itself may no longer feel right. The people may be difficult. Authority figures may seem unjust. Advancement may feel blocked. Compensation may feel inadequate.

These aren't just external problems. They're mirrors showing you where sanskars are active, where patterns are running, where you've given your power away.

Once, years ago, I didn't get a promotion I was certain I deserved. I had the seniority, the skills, the vision for the position. I walked into the interview confident and walked out certain I'd be chosen. When they gave the job to someone else, I was devastated.

For years afterward, I carried that defeat. I gossiped. I complained. I talked against my boss to anyone who would listen. I tried to make myself feel better by making the situation wrong, by making her wrong, by convincing others I'd been treated unfairly.

None of it helped. The pain metastasized.

What I was actually showing, though I couldn't see it then, was exactly why I wasn't ready for leadership. My reaction revealed the sanskar. I was so identified with needing the position, with needing external validation, that I couldn't observe what was happening with any clarity. I was the sanskar, not the soul witnessing it.

The Path That Actually Works

Eventually, I stopped reacting. Not because I suddenly became enlightened, but because I was meditating daily and I knew the behavior wasn't serving me. I pulled my attention inward.

This is where the work of karma begins. Not karma as punishment, but karma as responsibility.

First, stop the behavior that's making it worse. Stop gossiping. Stop complaining. Stop badmouthing anyone, even if you think you're justified. Every time you speak the complaint outward, you deepen the pattern. You're creating more karma, not resolving it.

Second, bring your attention to your actual feelings. Not the story about what happened or who was wrong. The feelings underneath. I had to feel the defeat, the hurt, the sense of being unseen. That took time. It took more than I wanted it to take.

Third, distinguish what you can change from what you can't. I couldn't change that they'd given the job to someone else. I could change how I showed up every day. I could change my relationships with colleagues. I could change what I was creating from where I was.

This is the critical shift. You stop trying to force external circumstances to match your expectations. You start aligning your internal state with your actual nature. Peace. Benevolence.

Nothing Outside You Has the Power

Here's the truth most people resist: nothing outside you can disempower you.

We don't want to believe this because it means taking responsibility. It's easier to point to the boss, the system, the unfairness, and say, "That's why I feel this way."

But disempowerment happens when you give your power away. When you decide that your peace depends on getting the promotion, on being recognized, on circumstances being different than they are.

The moment you make your internal state dependent on external conditions, you've lost your power. Not because someone took it. Because you handed it over.

I am a soul. My nature is peace.

That statement is either true regardless of circumstances, or it's not true at all. If your peace depends on getting what you want at work, you're not anchored in your spiritual identity.

You're anchored in the sanskar that says, "I need this external thing to be okay inside."

Empowerment comes from recognizing that your state of being belongs to you. You create it. You're responsible for it. And you can shift it regardless of what's happening around you.

What Shifts When You Shift

After I stopped reacting, after I worked through the feelings, I stayed in my job. I didn't leave. I decided to create what I actually wanted from where I was.

A few years later, an opportunity emerged. A new department was forming. I applied and was chosen. I became the first person in that department. There was no title, and it wasn't a formal leadership position, but it gave me the chance to shape everything from the beginning. To train everyone who came after. To create the culture and approach I'd always believed in.

I got exactly what I wanted. Not the external form I'd been attached to, but the actual essence. The ability to make an impact, to lead through example, to build something meaningful.

This is what happens when you shift internally. The external situation doesn't just stay the same while you feel better about it. The situation itself changes. The karma completes.

You know it's complete because the trigger no longer has power. You can look at the old situation without reactivity, without needing it to have been different. The sanskar has been witnessed, distinguished from your true self, and released.

Creating From Where You Are

The work environment isn't just where you earn money. It's where you practice being the soul observing the sanskars.

Every difficult colleague is an opportunity to notice where you're reactive. Every disappointment is a chance to see where you're attached. Every moment of feeling powerless is an invitation to reclaim your internal authority.

You don't need the title to have the impact. You don't need the recognition to create what matters. You need clarity about who you actually are and the willingness to show up from that place.

My relationships at work transformed. Not because anyone else changed, but because I stopped needing them to be different. I stopped reacting from the pattern and started responding from awareness. The same people who'd been difficult became collaborative. The same environment that felt oppressive became workable.

The shift was entirely internal. The results were entirely external.

The Peace That's Already There

Peace at work isn't about getting the right job, the right boss, the right circumstances. It's about making peace with yourself.

When you stop identifying with the need for external validation, when you stop making work mean something about your worth, when you recognize that you are the soul capable of witnessing all these patterns without being consumed by them, the peace that was always present becomes accessible.

This doesn't mean you stop caring about your work or stop wanting to advance. It means you stop suffering over it. You stop giving your power away to circumstances that were never meant to hold it.

You show up as the consciousness that can observe without drowning. That can feel disappointment without being defeated. That can experience setbacks without losing dignity.

The benevolent nature that's always been yours starts to shine through. Not because you built it or earned it, but because you stopped blocking it with attachment, reactivity, and identification with patterns that were never you.

Work becomes what it actually is: one environment where you practice being who you actually are.

Points for Contemplation

What have I made work mean beyond the actual agreement?

Where do I feel most powerless at work? Can I trace how I gave that power away?

What behavior am I engaging in that keeps the pattern alive?

Which aspect of work triggers the strongest reaction in me? What sanskar is that revealing?

What do I actually want to create or experience at work, beneath the need for external validation?

How would it feel to show up tomorrow as the soul observing my patterns rather than being consumed by them?

What would shift if I took full responsibility for my internal state regardless of external circumstances?

I Said No (And I'm Not Sorry)

T HE PATTERNS RUN DEEP. Apologizing constantly. Saying yes when you mean no. Staying on the phone when your body needs rest. Working overtime when you're already depleted. Making excuses when a simple "no" would suffice. These aren't just habits. They're sanskars, and they reveal something specific: a loss of spiritual self-respect.

If you recognize yourself in these patterns, what follows isn't about fixing your behavior. It's about excavation. You're learning to see the sanskar that believes you don't have the right to exist on your own terms.

When You Have No Boundaries

For years, I had a particular way of being with people. I would adjust to them completely, reacting and responding to whatever I perceived they needed. It was as if I had no self to assert. Just a collection of responses shaped by others' energy.

At the same time, I was judgmental and controlling. When I saw something wrong, I wanted to fix it, change it, manage it. These two patterns seem opposite, but they're connected. Both come from the same source: the sense of self has disappeared, and the sanskars are running the show.

Without boundaries, you lose track of where you end and others begin. You don't hold people accountable because you can't hold yourself accountable. I remember another nurse telling me once, frustrated: "You never hold anyone accountable for anything." I didn't understand what she meant. I was so immersed in emotional chaos that clarity was impossible.

Here's another symptom: I never took credit for my accomplishments. Someone else once said to me, "You have a doctorate and you act like you don't." That observation stayed with me. Why would someone who worked that hard refuse to acknowledge it?

The answer is fear. Fear of being alone. Fear of not being liked. Fear of what happens if I stand in my own dignity.

The sanskar believes that self-respect must be earned through others' approval. The soul knows better.

What "No" Actually Requires

To set a boundary when you've lived without them requires courage. You're going against momentum, against years of conditioning that say: disappear, adjust, apologize, explain.

Start small. Don't try to set boundaries with the most emotionally charged relationships first. Begin with something manageable. Maybe it's going to bed when you're tired instead of staying up to keep someone company. Maybe it's saying no to one volunteer commitment when you're overwhelmed.

The practice itself is simple: say no without apology or explanation.

I was at work once, completely overextended. My boss asked if I could do overtime. Usually, I would have said yes immediately, driven by the need to be seen as good, reliable, essential. Or I would have made excuses, kept talking, explained why I wanted to but couldn't.

This time I said: "No, thank you."

My boss paused, then said it was the best answer she'd ever heard to that question.

What made it different? The absence of apology. The absence of explanation. Just the simple truth: no, thank you.

This isn't anger. It's not defiance. It's self-respect emerging from soul consciousness. The soul doesn't need permission to exist. It doesn't need to justify its limits. When you say no from that place, you're not rejecting anyone. You're simply standing in what's true.

Two Territories

There are two landscapes you'll encounter as you practice this.

What others do

When you begin setting boundaries, people notice. If the relationships are healthy, they'll adjust. They might even feel relieved that you're taking care of yourself.

But sometimes people push back. They ask what's wrong. They seem upset. This isn't necessarily because you've done something wrong. It's because the system has changed, and systems resist change.

Remember: as long as you're not taking from anyone, you have the right to say no. You're not responsible for managing others' reactions to your self-respect.

What happens inside you

The first time you say no without apologizing, you might feel uncomfortable. The sanskar will protest. It will offer reasons why you should explain, should soften, should take it back.

Watch that impulse. Don't become it.

What you're cultivating is the capacity to witness the pattern without obeying it. You see the urge to apologize, and you let it pass. You feel the discomfort of standing your ground, and you stay anyway.

Underneath the discomfort, something else emerges: self-respect. Not the kind built on achievement or others' approval. The kind that comes from recognizing your own benevolent nature.

When you stop abandoning yourself, you discover you have more energy, not less. The depletion came from the constant self-betrayal, not from taking care of yourself.

The Spiritual Architecture

Boundaries aren't about becoming hard or protective. They're about clarity.

When you identify with the mind, with its fears and its need for approval, there's no center. You're reactive, scattered, always adjusting to external conditions. The sanskar that drives boundarylessness whispers: *if you say no, you'll be alone. If you assert yourself, you'll be rejected.*

But when you rest in soul consciousness, boundaries become natural. You recognize: I am a soul. I exist. I have inherent dignity. My nature is benevolent, peaceful, loving.

From that recognition, saying no isn't rejection. It's honesty. It's the kindest thing you can offer, because it's true.

Self-respect at the spiritual level means you stop waiting for others to validate your existence. You stop performing to earn the right to take up space. You simply are.

This is what the practice of saying no reveals. Each time you set a boundary without apology, you're distinguishing the soul from the sanskar. You're choosing truth over fear. You're standing in your own life.

The sanskar of people-pleasing will keep appearing. You don't need it to disappear. You need to stop letting it run your life. You become the witness, the soul observing the pattern, and in that observation, you find freedom.

Returning to Yourself

Real boundaries emerge when you stop trying to prove you deserve to exist. You already exist. You are a soul. Your nature is peace, loving, benevolent, pure, wise.

The sanskars convinced you otherwise. They taught you to apologize for taking up space, to explain your needs, to disappear so others could be comfortable. But those patterns were never you.

As you practice setting boundaries, you're not becoming someone new. You're clearing away what blocked your authentic self. The benevolent nature was always there. You just couldn't access it through the fear.

Each time you say no with quiet self-respect, you return to yourself a little more. The soul recognizes itself. The patterns lose their grip.

You don't transform by forcing change. You transform by taking responsibility for what's true, by witnessing your patterns with mercy, and by standing in your own dignity.

Points for Contemplation

Where in my life do I automatically say yes when I mean no?

What am I afraid will happen if I set a boundary?

What would it feel like to say "no, thank you" once this week without apologizing or explaining?

When I think about taking credit for my accomplishments, what stops me?

How does understanding myself as a soul change what boundaries mean?

Where have I been waiting for someone else to give me permission to take care of myself?

3

Emotional Rescue

Victory Over the Little Things

SOME CHANGES HAPPEN EASILY. You decide to do something differently and you simply do it. No struggle, no drama. But then there are other changes—the ones you've wanted to make for months or years, the ones you keep promising yourself you'll address, and yet they persist.

These are the patterns you know aren't serving you. Staying up too late scrolling through your phone when you need rest. Eating in ways that leave you feeling depleted. Reacting the same way in relationships even though you've promised yourself you won't. Thought loops that circle endlessly, creating stress you don't need.

These aren't extreme behaviors. They're not destroying your life. But they're not helping either. And despite your best intentions, despite knowing better, you keep doing them.

What makes these patterns so resistant to change? Why can't you just stop?

The answer is simpler than you might think: part of you doesn't want to.

The Force Behind the Pattern

Every behavior that persists has force behind it. There's a part of you that wants to change—the part that recognizes this isn't healthy, isn't loving, isn't aligned with how you want to live. But there's another part that wants to keep going. That part likes how the behavior makes you feel. It gets something from it.

Maybe you stay up late on screens because those hours feel like freedom after a day of demands. Maybe you eat certain foods because they provide comfort. Maybe you react in relationships because the reaction feels protective, even if it's not productive.

Both parts are real. The part that wants to change and the part that resists. Until you acknowledge both, you'll keep fighting yourself.

This is where most attempts at change fail. You try to force the shift. You use willpower, discipline, and harsh self-talk. You treat the resistant part like an enemy that needs to be overcome. But force creates resistance. The more you push, the more the pattern digs in.

What's needed instead is a different approach entirely. One that works with yourself rather than against yourself. One that's merciful rather than harsh.

Assessing Honestly Where You Are

Before you can change anything, you need to know what you're actually working with.

Pick one behavior you'd like to shift. Something specific. Not "I want to be healthier" but "I want to stop staying up past midnight on my phone." Not "I should be more patient" but "I want to stop snapping at my partner when I'm tired."

Now be honest with yourself about the force behind this pattern. Give yourself a percentage. How much of you actually wants to change this, and how much wants to keep doing it?

Maybe 80 percent wants to keep the pattern and 20 percent wants to change. Maybe it's 60-40. Maybe it's 90-10. Whatever the numbers are, be truthful. This is just you and you. No one else needs to know.

The goal isn't to judge those numbers. The goal is to see clearly what you're working with. Because if 80 percent of you wants to keep the pattern, trying to force immediate change will fail. What you need to do is gradually shift those percentages. Make the 20 grow and the 80 shrink.

This happens through understanding, not force.

The Process of Merciful Transformation

The first step is to observe without judgment. Tell the part of you that wants to keep the pattern: we're not going to change anything right now. I'm just going to watch.

This is merciful self-observation. You give yourself permission to continue the behavior while you simply notice. How does it make you feel? What happens before you do it? What happens after? You're not trying to fix anything. You're just watching with curiosity.

This removes the threat. The resistant part can relax because nothing is being taken away. And in that relaxation, you can actually see the pattern clearly.

Next, look at the past, present, and future of the behavior. Where did this pattern come from? Maybe you were exposed to something young and it became familiar. Maybe you learned this as a way of coping. Understanding the origin doesn't excuse the pattern, but it does help you see it with compassion rather than judgment.

Then look at what happens if you keep doing it. Not in a catastrophic way, but honestly. If you keep staying up too late, your body stays tired. If you keep reacting harshly in relationships, connection erodes. You're simply seeing the trajectory.

And finally, what would happen if you stopped? What's the actual benefit?

You're expanding your view. You're seeing the whole picture instead of just the moment of craving or habit.

As you do this, there may be feelings. Maybe a little grief when you realize how long you've been doing this, or how it's affected you. Maybe some sadness or loss. Allow that. Give yourself space for whatever emotional processing needs to happen. This is part of the healing.

Then articulate clearly what you want instead. Not what you should want. What you actually want. Be specific. "I want to go to bed at a reasonable time so I wake up rested and ready for morning meditation." "I want to eat in a way that makes my body feel good." "I want to respond to my partner with patience instead of irritation."

Say it to yourself. Write it down. Get clear on the intention.

Finding Middle Ground

Now comes the most important part: finding the middle ground. The place where change can happen without triggering resistance.

Think of it like this. If someone is eating chili burgers and fries every day and you tell them they have to completely change everything about how they eat, they won't do it. It feels too threatening. But if you suggest a hamburger with a salad instead, that's a shift they might actually make. It's not perfect, but it's movement in a better direction.

You need to find that same kind of shift for yourself. What change can you make that doesn't feel like deprivation or punishment? What adjustment feels workable?

Maybe you can't commit to being off screens by 6pm, but 9pm feels possible. Maybe you can't overhaul your entire diet, but you can add one healthy meal a day. Maybe you can't stop all reactive behavior, but you can pause for three breaths before responding.

Work with yourself. Negotiate. Find what feels like a reasonable step that honors both the part that wants to change and the part that's been resistant.

Then start the new pattern. Do it that day if you can. You're building precedent. You're showing yourself that change is possible, that it doesn't have to be painful.

And here's the thing: you can adjust. If the middle ground you chose doesn't work, shift it. This isn't about getting it perfect. It's about finding what actually works for you.

Why This Approach Works

Growing up, many of us learned that correction requires force. If something's wrong, you fix it with harshness, with anger, with willpower. But nothing actually needs to be changed that way.

Force creates resistance. Always. When you try to force yourself to stop a behavior, the pattern fights back. The heels dig in. The craving intensifies. You end up in a battle with yourself that exhausts you.

But when you work with yourself mercifully, when you observe without judgment and find middle ground that feels safe, resistance dissolves. The pattern begins to release naturally because you're not threatening it. You're inviting it to transform.

This is spiritual self-respect in action. You're treating yourself with the same patience and understanding you might offer a child learning something new. You're honoring your own process. You're trusting that change is possible without violence.

The Spiritual Foundation

This process connects directly to self-care and to your spiritual practice. When you learn to change behaviors mercifully, you're practicing the same awareness you bring to meditation. You're observing your mind without becoming lost in it. You're creating space between yourself as the soul and the patterns that arise.

The behaviors you're shifting aren't just about health or relationships or productivity. They're about living in alignment with your benevolent nature. They're about removing the obstacles between you and your authentic self.

When you can go to bed at a reasonable time, you wake rested for meditation. When you eat in ways that support your body, your energy stays clear. When you respond to others with patience instead of reactivity, love flows more naturally.

These aren't separate goals. They're all part of the same work: allowing your true nature to emerge by gently releasing what blocks it.

The process I've described might sound like psychology. In many ways it is. But what makes it spiritual is the foundation of merciful self-observation, the absence of judgment, and the recognition that everything has a reason for being there. You're not attacking yourself. You're not trying to become someone new. You're easing yourself into patterns you feel good about, patterns that reflect who you actually are.

This takes practice. The more you use this approach, the more behaviors transform naturally. Not through force, but through understanding. Not through harshness, but through mercy.

You are learning to guide yourself with the same benevolence you're learning to recognize as your nature. The soul caring for itself. The consciousness directing the mind with clarity and compassion.

Points for Contemplation

What behavior would I like to change that has been resisting change?

Honestly, what percentage of me wants to change and what percentage wants to stay the same?

Where did this pattern come from? What purpose has it served?

What specifically do I want instead?

What middle ground can I find that doesn't feel threatening to either part of myself?

Can I observe this pattern for a few days without trying to change it, simply watching with curiosity?

Finishing Anger

MOST OF US THINK anger is a problem to solve. We try to manage it, redirect it, or justify why we had every right to feel it. But how often do we stop to ask ourselves what anger costs us spiritually?

Not what it costs in relationships, though that's real. Not what it costs in health, though that matters. What does it cost us in terms of our connection to our own benevolent nature?

When you sit in meditation and remember "I am a soul, my nature is peace," and then an hour later find yourself angry at traffic, at a coworker, at yourself, something is revealed. The anger is information that shows you where you've been identified with a sanskar rather than standing as the soul.

This chapter is about finishing that pattern. Not suppressing it or pretending it doesn't exist, but distinguishing yourself from it so completely that it loses its power over you.

The Mechanism of Anger

Anger appears when we believe circumstances *should* be different than they are. Someone should have called back.

The meeting should have gone another way. People should understand what we need without being told.

The word "should" is the signal. Every time you think something should be other than it is, you're setting yourself up for anger.

Notice this carefully. The anger isn't caused by what happened. It's caused by your belief about what should have happened. The circumstance simply revealed the belief you were already carrying.

I spent years righteously angry at people who disappointed me. Someone would cancel plans and I'd think, "They should have respected my time." The anger felt justified, even noble. I was standing up for myself, wasn't I?

But when I looked more closely in meditation, when I observed without judgment, I saw something else. The anger wasn't protecting me. It was draining me. Every time I became angry, I gave away a little more of my spiritual self-respect.

Some people use anger to try to control circumstances, to dominate, to manipulate. They think anger is how you get what you want, how you get things done. But that kind of anger is desperation disguised as strength. It's the opposite of spiritual self-respect. It causes suffering to yourself and others, which means it cannot be spiritual.

Anything that creates sorrow, to yourself or to another, is not spiritual, not grounded in your benevolent nature.

A Necessary Distinction

There's a difference between anger as reaction and the firm clarity that establishes a boundary.

Sometimes what we call anger is actually self-respect reasserting itself. You recognize something isn't working. You need to make a change. You speak clearly, set a limit, walk away from what's harmful. There's energy in that moment, yes. But it's not the hot, reactive anger we're talking about in this chapter. It's taking care of yourself.

That kind of anger doesn't create suffering. It doesn't deplete you. It doesn't require circumstances to be different than they are. It simply recognizes what is and responds from spiritual self-respect.

The anger this chapter addresses is different. It's resistance. Loss of control. The kind that leaves you exhausted, that damages your internal peace, that makes you feel powerless even when you're trying to assert power.

Pay attention to the difference in your own experience. When you set a boundary from clarity, you feel stable afterward. When you react from anger, you feel drained.

One is you, the soul, acting from self- respect. The other is the sanskar taking over.

What Anger Actually Costs

Anger depletes internal power. This is not the loud, forceful kind of power that dominates a room. In this context, I mean the quiet kind of power, the spiritual kind, the capacity to remain stable regardless of what's happening around you.

Think of someone you know who seems genuinely unshakeable. Not because they suppress their feelings, but because they don't need circumstances to be different than they are. That quality comes from spiritual self-respect, from standing firmly as the soul rather than being tossed around by reactions.

Every time you become angry, you're saying: this external thing has more power over me than my own internal state. You've handed control to the circumstance.

For years I never understood Western movies. Men standing in the street, staring at each other, waiting to see who moves first. It seemed pointless. Then I realized what they're actually about. Self-respect. Who has the most. Who can remain most uninfluenced by what's happening around them.

The question for you is the same. Do you remain stable when circumstances shift? Or do you react, lose your center, feel powerless?

Anger is the signal that you've lost connection to your spiritual identity. You've become the sanskar instead of the soul observing it.

Where the Pattern Began

Most anger patterns were formed early, when you actually were powerless. When you were a child and couldn't control what happened to you, anger became a way to signal distress, to try to influence adults, to express the frustration of having no agency.

My father carried anger everywhere. It shaped how he moved through the world, how he spoke, how he responded to difficulty. I absorbed that pattern without choosing it. For years I expressed anger the same way he did because I'd learned that's what you do when you feel powerless.

The sanskar isn't who you are. It's what you picked up. And when you can see that clearly, when you can distinguish between the soul and the accumulated pattern, you stop defending the anger. You stop justifying it. You simply observe: this is a pattern appearing. I am not that pattern. I am the consciousness aware of it.

The Practice of Merciful Observation

This is where the work actually happens. Not in understanding anger intellectually, but in catching it as it appears and choosing to witness rather than become it.

Start by noticing when you're already angry. After the fact. You reacted, you felt the heat, the righteousness, the conviction that you were right. Later, in meditation or in quiet, you recognize: that was the sanskar.

This is the first stage.

As your practice deepens, you'll catch it earlier. You'll feel the irritation rising and simultaneously think: this is the pattern. You're both experiencing it and observing it. The distinction is beginning.

Eventually, you'll notice the trigger before the anger fully activates. Someone cancels plans and instead of becoming angry, you watch the impulse arise. You see the belief—"they should have respected my time"—and recognize it as thought, not truth. The anger doesn't take hold because you've distinguished yourself from it.

This doesn't happen overnight. Some anger patterns will take years of patient observation. And that's fine. You're not racing toward perfection. You're developing a capacity to witness yourself with clarity and mercy.

When I notice anger now, I get curious. What belief is underneath this? What am I making this circumstance mean about me? Where did I give my power away?

The questions aren't harsh. They're genuine investigation. I'm watching the mechanism with interest, the way you'd watch anything you want to understand.

Accessing What Lies Beneath

Underneath every anger pattern is your benevolent nature, waiting.

When you distinguish yourself from anger, when you can observe it without becoming it, you naturally access kindness. Patience. Understanding. Not because you've worked to become those things, but because that's what you actually are when you're not identified with the pattern.

This is spiritual self-respect: the recognition of your own benevolent capacity, independent of whether circumstances go your way.

The anger told you that your peace depended on things being different. Meditation teaches you the opposite. Your peace is constant. Your nature is benevolent. Circumstances reveal whether you're connected to that truth or lost in reaction.

Every time you witness anger without becoming it, you reclaim a little more of your spiritual power. You stop needing the world to behave. You stop exhausting yourself trying to control what you can't control.

Your spiritual nature emerges again, stable and clear, capable of response rather than reaction.

Points for Contemplation

When do I feel most justified in my anger?

What belief is underneath that anger—what "should" am I holding?

Can I recall a moment when anger cost me my internal peace, even though I felt right?

Where did I first learn that anger was an appropriate response to feeling powerless?

What would it feel like to witness anger arising without becoming it?

Which situation in my life right now is inviting me to practice this distinction?

Can I observe my anger patterns this week with curiosity rather than judgment?

Facing Overwhelm

THE PROBLEM OF OVERWHELM seems circumstantial: too many responsibilities, too many people depending on us, too little time. But then we have to ask ourselves: why does the same situation leave one person steady and another person drowning?

When I look closely at my own experience with overwhelm, I see something unexpected. The circumstances that triggered it were often minor. A computer not working. An unexpected phone call. Someone asking me to do one more thing. These weren't catastrophes. They were ordinary moments in an ordinary life.

Yet in those moments, I felt completely helpless. And this brings us to the essential distinction that overwhelm is helplessness wearing a different name.

The Pattern Beneath the Surface

Helplessness is a sanskar. It lives in the mind as a feeling that convinces you: "I can't handle this. I don't know what to do. Everything is too much."

The mind loops. Three tasks become thirty in your thoughts. You replay the same concerns without resolution. The feeling of pressure builds, but nothing actually gets done. You're spinning, caught in the pattern, identified with it completely.

Think about someone balancing plates on sticks, keeping eight spinning at once. That was me. I managed everything, held everything together, and the moment something unexpected appeared, I couldn't take it. The whole structure felt ready to collapse.

What I didn't realize then was that the structure wasn't real. The overwhelm wasn't caused by the tasks. It was caused by my relationship to them, my underlying belief that I was powerless.

I remember my mother during a particularly stressful time when she was completing her doctorate. Papers covered every surface in the house. Her system was visual, everything spread out where she could see it. To anyone else it looked chaotic, but for her it worked.

Until it didn't.

One day she became overwhelmed. Not by the dissertation itself, but by a pen left in the wrong place. She exploded at my father over this pen, this tiny detail. That's how overwhelm operates. It's not proportional. It's not logical. It attaches to whatever is nearest when the feeling takes over.

The real issue was never the pen. The real issue was the feeling of helplessness underneath, waiting for a reason to justify itself.

When You Don't Know You Have Choices

Helplessness lives as a belief that you have no options. You must do everything. You must handle everything. You must manage everyone's needs. The concept of choice doesn't even enter your awareness.

For years, I didn't know I could say no. I didn't know I could postpone something. I didn't know I could stop entirely if needed.

This is where having a calm, linear-minded person around becomes essential. My husband would watch me spiral and ask simple questions. "Do you have to do that now? Could you do it tomorrow? What if you just didn't do it at all?"

Those questions revealed options I couldn't see. The overwhelm had convinced me there was only one way forward: push through, handle everything, somehow manage it all.

But there are always choices. Always.

The soul knows this. The soul, your true self, is inherently capable. It can observe, distinguish, decide. But when you're identified with the sanskar of helplessness, you lose access to that capacity. You become the pattern instead of the consciousness witnessing it.

The First Act of Power

This sounds too simple to matter, but writing it down is the first real act of power against helplessness. When you put pen to paper and list what needs to be done, you immediately take a different position. You're no longer drowning in the mental loop. You're observing it from outside.

The list itself reveals the truth. Some things are urgent. Some can wait. Some don't actually need to happen at all. But you can't see this while the tasks circle in your mind, each one feeling equally impossible.

Writing externalizes what was internal. It gives form to what felt formless. And in that simple act, you begin to distinguish yourself from the overwhelm.

You realize: I have a pen. I have paper. I'm writing. I'm not helpless.

This is spiritual practice disguised as practicality. You're training the intellect to take charge, to organize, to see clearly. You're remembering that you are the soul, the one capable of observation and decision, not the swirling thoughts claiming you can't handle this.

Standing in Your Own Power

The next realization is even more radical: you don't have to do everything today.

When you're identified with helplessness, time collapses. Everything feels immediate. Everything feels urgent. The mind says: "This must be done now and this and this and this."

But once the emotions are in check, your spiritual powers of discernment and decision making can come forth to help. With these powers, I can prioritize. I can say: "Today this matters. Tomorrow that can happen. Next week is soon enough for the rest."

This isn't procrastination. This is discernment.

I learned something else from watching how naturally some people set boundaries. They can cut things off completely. If something isn't working, they stop. No drama, no guilt. Just a clear decision.

I remember the day I nearly threw my computer in the lake. The computer wasn't cooperating. That familiar feeling started rising, the helplessness, the sense of being at the mercy of circumstances. And I told myself: "I will throw this in the lake. I will not be dominated by a machine."

I didn't actually throw it. But threatening to changed something inside me. I was taking a stand. I was saying: "I have the power here. Not the computer. Not the circumstance. Me."

This is what it means to stop being dominated. Not dominated by tasks, by technology, by other people's expectations, by your own body's limitations. You always have the choice to say no, to stop, to walk away.

That choice is spiritual power. It's self-respect at the most fundamental level.

Returning to Yourself

Overwhelm, at its deepest level, is forgetting who you are.

You forget that you are the soul, fundamentally peaceful, fundamentally capable. You forget that your benevolent nature and innate wisdom are already present, already accessible. You identify with the pattern of helplessness instead.

Eventually, through the practice of mediation, the pattern appears but doesn't take you over. You see the situation that would normally trigger overwhelm, and instead of becoming helpless, you watch the impulse arise and pass. You remain yourself.

This isn't about never feeling pressure or stress. It's about not losing yourself to it. It's about maintaining the awareness that you are the consciousness observing the pressure, not the pressure itself.

That awareness is freedom.

I've come a long way with this. The overwhelm that used to control my life is mostly gone now. Not because my circumstances became easier, but because I learned to distinguish myself from the pattern. I learned to take responsibility without indulging in helplessness. I learned to stand in my own power.

You can too. But it requires honesty. It requires looking at yourself without judgment and admitting: "Yes, I do this. Yes, this is my pattern."

And then it requires practice. Daily meditation to reinforce your spiritual identity. Daily observation to catch the pattern when it appears. Daily choices to respond differently.

Little by little, you reclaim yourself.

Points for Contemplation

When does the feeling of helplessness arise in my life? What situations or people trigger it most often?

Do I communicate clearly when I need help, or do I express overwhelm as blame or frustration?

What would it feel like to write down everything I think I must do and recognize that I don't have to do it all today?

Where have I been dominated by circumstances, tasks, or other people's expectations when I actually had the power to say no?

What choices do I have right now that I haven't been allowing myself to see?

Facing Exhaustion

YOU KNOW THE FEELING. You've slept enough. You've rested. Maybe you even took time off. But when you sit down to begin your day, there's a heaviness that has nothing to do with your body.

This isn't the tiredness that comes from physical exertion or lack of sleep. This is something else entirely. A weariness that lives deeper, that no amount of rest seems to touch.

You might have tried to explain it away. Stress. Too much on your plate. The demands of life. And perhaps those things contribute. But if you're honest, you sense something more fundamental at work.

This exhaustion isn't physical. It's spiritual. And it's trying to tell you something.

The Exhaustion Your Body Can't Explain

Physical tiredness has a clear cause and a clear remedy. You worked hard, you rest. You didn't sleep enough, you sleep more. The body recovers when given what it needs.

Spiritual exhaustion works differently. It comes from living at a distance from yourself, from maintaining versions of who you think you should be rather than resting in who you are. It's the tiredness of performing, of holding up facades, of managing how others perceive you.

You can feel it distinctly if you pay attention. Physical tiredness settles in the body. Spiritual tiredness lives deeper. It's a heaviness in your consciousness, a sense that you're carrying something invisible but constant.

The soul doesn't tire from genuine action. It tires from inauthenticity.

When you live disconnected from your true nature, when you operate primarily from sanskars rather than soul awareness, every interaction costs energy. You're maintaining something that isn't real. And maintenance is exhausting.

What We Maintain That Drains Us

For years, I tried to be perfect. Not consciously, but the pattern was there. I wanted to appear capable, together, spiritually advanced. I wanted people to see me as someone who had it figured out.

The exhaustion was constant. Not because I was doing too much, though I was, but because I was performing. Every conversation, every interaction carried this invisible weight: maintain the image, don't let them see the struggle, keep the façade intact.

I didn't realize how much energy that cost until I began to observe it. In meditation, sitting quietly with "I am a soul,"

I could feel the gap between my peaceful nature and the constructed self I was maintaining. The difference was stark.

The persona I'd built wasn't protecting me. It was draining me.

Most of us do this in some form. We maintain versions of ourselves we think we need to be. The capable one who never struggles. The generous one who never needs anything. The strong one who doesn't feel pain. The spiritual one who's always peaceful.

These aren't bad intentions. But they're exhausting to sustain because they're not true. You are a soul. Your nature is already benevolent, already peaceful. The moment you try to construct those qualities from the outside, through behavior and image, you begin to tire.

The Signal in Your Weariness

Exhaustion isn't the enemy. It's feedback.

When you feel bone-tired for no physical reason, your consciousness is telling you something. Look at what you're maintaining. Notice where you're performing rather than being. Pay attention to the gap between who you actually are and who you're trying to appear to be.

This requires your intellect, the part of you capable of clear observation. Not the mind that races and reacts, but the calm, witnessing awareness that can look honestly at your patterns.

Sit with these questions. Where do I feel most depleted? What situations drain me? Which relationships leave me exhausted? Not to blame anyone or fix anything, but simply to see clearly.

Often you'll notice the exhaustion comes not from the situation itself but from how you're showing up in it. You're managing perceptions. You're holding back truth. You're maintaining an image that requires constant energy.

The intellect can distinguish this. It can recognize: this exhaustion is spiritual, not physical. I'm tired because I'm not being authentic here.

The Return to Sustainable Energy

Energy returns when you stop performing.

This isn't about suddenly dropping all your responsibilities or relationships. It's about beginning to observe where you're living from construction rather than from truth, and gently, mercifully, letting the construction dissolve.

In meditation, you practice this return. You sit quietly and remember: I am a soul. My nature is peace. Not "I should be peaceful" or "I want to appear peaceful," but "peace is already what I am."

That remembrance costs nothing. It requires no maintenance. You're not building something or trying to become something. You're simply resting in what's true.

As you practice this, you begin to notice the difference in daily life. There are moments when you're living from your authentic nature and moments when you're performing. The authentic moments feel lighter, even when they're challenging. The performed moments feel heavy, even when they're pleasant.

Your self-respect begins to shift. Real self-respect, spiritual self-respect, comes from recognizing your benevolent nature.

Not from how well you perform or how others perceive you, but from knowing what you actually are.

When you give from that place, you don't deplete. When you work from that place, you don't exhaust yourself. The action itself becomes an expression of your nature rather than a construction you're maintaining.

This doesn't mean life becomes effortless. Bodies still tire. Circumstances still challenge. But the spiritual exhaustion, that deep weariness that rest can't touch, begins to lift.

Points for Contemplation

Where am I maintaining a version of myself that isn't completely true?

What would shift if I stopped managing how others perceive me in one specific relationship?

Can I distinguish the weight of performance from the ease of authentic action in my daily life?

When I sit in meditation and remember "I am a soul," what gap do I notice between that truth and how I've been living?

What does my spiritual exhaustion want me to see about myself?

Facing Disappointment

WE DIDN'T GET THE job. The relationship ended. The opportunity fell through. When circumstances don't go our way, we wrestle with feelings of disappointment. But spiritually speaking, we need to consider a deeper disappointment: the persistent sense that something is fundamentally wrong, not with your circumstances, but with y ou.

I once described this feeling as being like a beautiful apple. From the outside, everything looks perfect, shiny, put together. But when you bite into it, the inside is rotten. Does that mean you're rotten? No. But that's what this kind of disappointment feels like. Day after day, you try your best. You do everything you're supposed to do. And by the end of the day, you still don't feel good about yourself. You still feel that ache.

If you recognize this feeling, if you've carried it for years despite external success, you've already discovered something important: conventional advice about managing expectations or reframing disappointment doesn't touch this level. Because this isn't about circumstances. This is about the absence of spiritual self-respect.

The Disappointment No One Discusses

Everyone acknowledges grief after loss. Everyone understands feeling disappointed when something specific goes wrong. But this other thing, this daily waking up and trying again and still feeling empty by evening, this is what people don't talk about except in the language of depression.

I'm not talking about clinical depression here. I'm talking about the specific feeling of internal disappointment that persists regardless of what you achieve or how well you perform. The exhaustion of looking good on the outside while suffering quietly on the inside.

Years ago, I didn't get a job I was certain I would get, one I was genuinely qualified for. The disappointment was devastating. It took me five years to fully recover emotionally from that experience because of how deeply I had invested my sense of self in that outcome. I had placed all my worth in that one external thing.

Looking back, I can see the pattern. I was operating from a place of such low self-respect that any external rejection felt like confirmation of what I already believed about myself. The circumstance didn't create the devastation. My lack of internal foundation did.

Where Experience Actually Happens

Think of your experience as happening on three levels.

The outer layer is everything that's happening around you. Events, circumstances, other people's responses, outcomes you can't control. This layer is constantly changing.

The middle layer is your mind and emotional landscape. This is where you react to the outer layer, where feelings rise and fall, where thoughts spin and multiply. Most of us live here, constantly responding to what's happening outside.

The deepest layer is you, the soul. Your nature is peace. Your nature is loving and benevolent. This layer doesn't change. But if you don't know it exists, if you've never experienced it directly, you have no choice but to stay in that middle layer, reacting.

When I only know the middle layer, when that's my entire reality, I'm completely at the mercy of external events. Something goes wrong outside, I feel terrible inside. Something goes right outside, I feel temporarily better. But there's no stability. No real peace. Just constant reaction.

This is why disappointment becomes persistent. You're trying to build self-respect from circumstances instead of from consciousness itself.

Building From the Inside Out

Raja Yoga meditation works differently than most approaches to inner work. You're not trying to fix your thoughts or manage your feelings. You're not analyzing why you feel disappointed or working to reframe the disappointment into something positive.

You're establishing a new center of identification.

Each morning, you sit quietly and remind yourself of the truth. I am a soul. My nature is peace. I am living consciousness working through this body. My nature is loving and benevolent. These aren't affirmations you're trying to believe. They're truths you're remembering.

When you practice this daily, something shifts in that middle layer where all the pain lives. The mind begins to have a choice. Before, it could only react to external events because that was all it knew. Now there's another reference point. The peaceful soul. The loving consciousness that exists regardless of circumstances.

This doesn't happen instantly. But gradually, the experience of peace becomes real. The knowledge that you are fundamentally benevolent becomes felt truth rather than just concept. And as this internal foundation strengthens, external events lose their power to devastate you.

You might still feel natural disappointment when something doesn't work out. But you won't collapse internally. You won't spend five years recovering from not getting a job. Because your self-respect isn't dependent on getting the job anymore.

The Voice That Undermines Everything

There's something else that has to be addressed if you're going to heal this deep disappointment. The negative self-talk. The internal voice that criticizes and diminishes you.

This is perhaps the worst poison in the mind because it directly attacks the foundation you're trying to build. You can meditate each morning, reminding yourself that you're a peaceful soul, but if you spend the rest of the day telling yourself you're worthless, stupid, not good enough, the meditation can't take root.

From the beginning of spiritual practice, you have to set a boundary with this voice. Not tolerate it. Not engage with it or try to reason with it. Simply refuse to allow it space.

Think of it as standing up to a bully. The bully doesn't stop because you explain why bullying is wrong. The bully stops when you refuse to be bullied. When you stand your ground.

For me, this took time. The critical voice didn't disappear immediately. But each time it appeared, I would notice it and redirect. That's not true. That's not who I am. The voice gradually lost its power. Eventually, it stopped appearing altogether.

This matters because self-respect and self-criticism cannot coexist. If you're serious about building spiritual self-respect, about establishing yourself in soul consciousness, you have to stop participating in your own diminishment.

Points for Contemplation

When I feel disappointed, is it about the circumstance or about myself?

What does the voice in my mind say to me throughout the day?

Can I feel the difference between the peaceful soul I am and the disappointed reactions I experience?

Where have I been looking for self-respect from external sources when only I can build it from within?

What would it mean to witness my disappointment with mercy rather than identifying with it?

Facing Illness

WHEN THE BODY BECOMES ill, something shifts in how we relate to ourselves. The routines we depend on fall away. The identity we've built around capability or independence suddenly feels fragile. We discover how much we've been identifying with the body's performance, its reliability, its cooperation with our plans.

Illness doesn't just disrupt the body. It reveals where we've been living unconsciously, where our sense of self depends on circumstances staying stable.

The body will do what the body does. It ages, becomes injured, develops conditions. That's its nature. But you, the soul, remain constant beneath all of it. The question isn't how to avoid the body's reality. The question is: can you remain connected to your true nature while the body experiences what it experiences?

What the Body Is Going Through

There are many forms of illness. Some arrive suddenly, a cold or flu that disrupts a week. Others come from injury, an accident that changes mobility overnight. Some conditions run in families, patterns written into the body's design before you had any choice. Others develop from how we've lived, the accumulated effect of choices made when we didn't know better or didn't care enough.

And some illnesses become chronic companions, conditions that reshape daily life permanently.

Each type asks something different of us. But the invitation is always the same: to distinguish yourself from what the body is experiencing. To recognize that while the body goes through its process, you remain the consciousness observing it.

When my son had a seizure as a baby, I remember feeling grateful to be a nurse. Not because I could fix it, but because I understood what was happening. Knowledge didn't stop my adrenaline or erase the fear of seeing my child in distress. But it gave me the ability to remain present, to respond rather than panic, to know that what looked terrifying would pass.

That distinction between what's happening and who I am while it's happening is what we're learning here.

The Four Movements of Response

When illness appears, there are four levels where response happens. Most people get stuck at one level and wonder why they suffer more than the circumstance requires.

Seeking Physical Care
The first responsibility is simple: find out what's actually happening. Go to the doctor. Get the tests. Use the knowledge available. This isn't about blind faith in any particular

system. It's about being responsible enough to gather accurate information.

Some people resist this out of fear or distrust. But not knowing doesn't protect you. It just keeps you in a fog of anxiety, imagining possibilities instead of dealing with what is.

Building Emotional Clarity

Once you know what's happening physically, the next level is understanding. What is this condition? How does it work? What happens now?

Education is medicine for the emotional level. Fear grows in ignorance. The more you understand, the less power fear has over your emotional state. You're not pretending everything is fine. You're getting clear about what's actually true so your emotions can respond to reality instead of imagination.

Developing Psychological Acceptance

This is where most people get stuck because this is where the real suffering lives. Not in the body's pain but in the mind's rejection of what's happening.

I had a classmate in nursing school who was intensely capable, someone who built her identity around being active and self-sufficient. She slipped on ice, broke her leg in three places, and had to spend two months in traction, completely immobilized. She told me later that during those months, she had thoughts of ending her life. Not because of physical pain. Because she couldn't tolerate the loss of who she thought she was

.

That's psychological suffering. The body was healing. But her mind was at war with reality.

This level asks for the capacity to tolerate what is. Not in the sense of gritting your teeth and enduring. Tolerance, spiritually understood, means accepting reality fully without internal resistance.

It means saying: this is happening. I don't have to like it, but I'm not going to exhaust myself fighting what already is.

Behind that acceptance is understanding. Of course this upsets me. Of course I wish it were different. But wishing doesn't change what's true. The generous attitude toward yourself isn't pretending you're fine. It's acknowledging the difficulty while refusing to add mental warfare on top of it.

Practicing Spiritual Restoration

The fourth level is where meditation becomes essential. This is the practice of withdrawing into soul consciousness, giving your body what I call a break from your mental activity.

When you sit quietly and remember, "I am a soul, my nature is peace," you're actually shifting the body's chemistry. You're not identified with the body's condition. You're the consciousness observing it, the awareness that remains peaceful regardless of what the body experiences.

This isn't escapism. It's strategic. The body heals better when peaceful vibrations move through it rather than stress and fear. You already know this is true. You've felt how anxiety tightens everything, how worry makes pain worse.

The bodiless stage is deliberate medicine. For even a few minutes, you stop being the person with the illness and become the soul witnessing an experience. That distinction creates space. And in that space, healing becomes possible.

The Hidden Work of Acceptance

Why is psychological acceptance so difficult? Because illness confronts us with loss. Loss of control, loss of capability, loss of the identity we've built around what the body can do.

The mind wants to bargain. If I do this, will it go away? It wants to be angry. Why is this happening to me? It moves through denial, depression, resistance. All of this is the mind trying to reject what already is.

But here's what's true: saying "I don't want this" doesn't make it stop. The only thing that statement does is create suffering on top of the circumstance.

Acceptance isn't resignation. It's power. When you can look directly at what's happening and say, "This is the reality I'm working with," you stop wasting energy on internal warfare. All that energy becomes available for actual response.

You're learning to face what is. Not to fix your feelings about it. Not to think your way into being okay with it. Just to be present with reality as it actually appears.

What Remains When Everything Shifts

Two people can have the same diagnosis and suffer completely differently. The difference isn't in the body. It's in the relationship to what's happening.

One person identifies completely with the condition. They become "the sick person," and their entire sense of self revolves around managing, fearing, or fighting the illness.

Another person experiences the same condition but remains connected to something deeper. They know: this is what the body is going through. I am the soul caring for this body while it experiences this process.

That distinction changes everything. Not because the illness disappears. Because the suffering decreases.

When you practice soul consciousness regularly, when you sit each morning and remember your benevolent nature, you build the capacity to remain steady regardless of circumstances. The body's condition stops defining your worth or your peace.

Illness becomes a teacher when you stop resisting it as an enemy. The body goes through what it goes through. Your work is to remain connected to the truth of who you are while it does.

Points for Contemplation

When illness appears, what is my first response—fear, rejection, or curiosity?

Can I seek medical care without letting fear dominate my emotional state?

Where am I fighting reality by thinking "I don't want this" instead of acknowledging "this is what's happening"?

Do I identify with the body's condition or remain aware that I am the soul witnessing an experience?

What would it mean to care for my body with understanding rather than remain caught in frustration when it doesn't cooperate?

Facing Grief

I F YOU'VE LOST SOMEONE, you know the feeling of grief. You focus on their absence, the loss, what you'll miss. A space has opened up that wasn't there before. And into that space comes everything—sadness, confusion, sometimes anger, sometimes a strange emptiness that nothing seems to fi ll.

This isn't just emotional pain. It's a shift in consciousness itself.

The Empty Space

Think of your consciousness as territory, like an acre of land. The people you love occupy space in that territory. Your mother might occupy a quarter of it. Your partner, another portion. Your closest friend, a section over there.

You don't usually notice this. The space feels full, occupied, integrated into how you experience yourself and your life.

When someone dies, that space doesn't disappear. It remains, but now it's empty. And you feel it. You feel the absence as intensely as you once felt the presence.

This is what grief actually is. Not just missing someone, but the lived experience of empty space inside your own consciousness.

Some people respond to this emptiness by questioning everything. What's the purpose of life? Why does anything matter? These questions arise because the loss is felt internally, in the self. When a significant portion of your inner territory suddenly empties, it destabilizes your sense of meaning.

Others fill the space quickly with blame. They blame God, circumstances, doctors, themselves. The mind rushes to make sense of what feels senseless.

And some people simply allow the space to remain empty while they grieve. They feel what they feel without rushing to resolve it or make it mean something.

All of these responses are human. If you're grieving, whatever you're feeling is real and valid. The people around you may grow impatient. They may ask why you're not "over it" after months or years. But they're not experiencing your inner territory. They don't feel the space that person occupied. You do.

What Never Dies

Here's what changes everything: the soul never dies.

The body is left behind. The physical form you knew, the voice, the presence in the room—that ends. But consciousness itself continues. The soul, the essential being of the person you loved, doesn't stop existing just because the body stopped functioning.

This isn't wishful thinking. It's spiritual law.

I experienced this when my mother passed three years ago. We were very close. I had time to prepare because she had cancer, but preparation doesn't eliminate the reality of loss. When I stood at her memorial, I expected to feel devastated. Instead, I felt two things: profound gratitude and the unmistakable sense that she wasn't gone.

I told my family that I didn't feel like she was gone. It wasn't denial. It was awareness. The relationship we had, the love, the influence she had on my life, none of that disappeared when her body did.

My husband Ken had a similar experience. His mother died in childbirth when he was sixteen. He was there when she was transported to the hospital. He prayed she would survive. When she was pronounced dead on arrival, he went into shock. But even in that shock, he felt something clear: she was still there. Not physically, but present and connected.

He had no spiritual framework for this at the time. He didn't know about soul consciousness or the eternal nature of the self. But he felt it anyway. And that feeling sustained him through years of responsibility as the eldest son, caring for siblings, watching his father struggle.

Decades later, when his sister passed at fifty-five, he felt the same thing. He held her hand while she was on life support. He sensed she was ready to go, that she was okay. And when she died, he didn't feel she had gone somewhere terrible or ceased to exist. He felt her continuation.

These aren't isolated experiences. Near-death research documents this phenomenon repeatedly. People whose hearts stop during cardiac arrest, who are clinically dead and then revived, often report the same experience: consciousness continuing, a sense of light, sometimes meeting deceased loved ones, and above all, a pleasant atmosphere. These reports come from people of different religious backgrounds, including those with no religious beliefs at all.

The doctors studying this—cardiologists and neurosurgeons investigating ways to preserve brain function after heart attacks—were baffled. How could people report detailed, coherent experiences when their brains had no measurable activity?

Because consciousness doesn't depend on the brain. The brain is an instrument the soul uses, but the soul itself is independent. When the body fails, the soul continues.

This understanding doesn't eliminate grief. But it can help prevent despair.

What Remains

When the body is gone, what's left?

Everything that matters.

The memories you share are eternal. They don't disappear when someone dies. They remain, vivid and alive, part of your consciousness. When you remember your mother's laugh or your friend's particular way of seeing things, you're accessing something real. Not a recording of the past, but a living memory that continues to shape you.

The influence they had on your life doesn't end. The ways they taught you to think, the values they modeled, the love they gave you—all of that continues to work in you. They live on through their impact.

And the relationship itself transcends physical presence. This is the part that's hardest to explain but easiest to feel. When you think of someone you loved, you're not just remembering. You're connecting. There's an interaction happening, soul to soul, across the boundary of physical death.

In Ken's culture, when someone dies, people gather for thirteen nights to sing spiritual songs and share knowledge about the soul. At his sister's memorial, he spoke about this—how each soul is unique, formed by their experiences during life, and how the relationship continues if there's love and gratitude rather than suffering and blame.

People came up to him afterward and said it helped them. Why? Because it's true. Because somewhere inside, we already know this. We just need permission to trust what we feel.

Transforming Grief Into Connection

You don't have to stop feeling grief. You don't have to pretend you're fine or rush toward acceptance.

But you can transform grief into something that heals both you and the person who's gone.

Start with gratitude. Not forced positivity, but genuine acknowledgment of what you received. When my mother died, I stood in front of my family and felt overwhelming gratitude—for her example, her companionship, everything she gave me. That feeling, that genuine appreciation, I believe reached her. Because I wasn't having the feeling in isolation. I was having it while remembering her, while connected to her through memory and love.

When memories arise, and they will, send love. Not as a technique, but as a natural expression of what you feel. Let the memory become a bridge rather than a wound. Instead of thinking "I miss them" and stopping there in pain, think "I'm grateful for them" and let that gratitude move toward them.

This isn't about fixing your grief or making it go away. It's about using your consciousness intentionally. You have a choice in how you meet the memories. You can meet them with bitterness and pain, or you can meet them with love and gratitude. Both responses acknowledge the loss. But one keeps you trapped in suffering, and the other creates healing.

The empty space in your consciousness doesn't have to remain empty forever. It can fill with something different than what was there before. Not a replacement—nothing replaces the person you lost. But the space can become sacred territory, a place where love and gratitude live, where your connection to that person continues in a new form.

This is spiritual practice. This is using your consciousness to transform suffering into something that serves both you and them.

The Soul Observing

Here, in the midst of grief, you're learning something deeper. You're learning to be the soul observing even your grief. You feel the pain—you're not pretending it doesn't exist. But you're also aware that you're feeling it. You're the consciousness witnessing the empty space, the sadness, the longing.

This distinction doesn't remove the feeling. But it prevents the feeling from overwhelming you completely. You're not your grief. You're the soul experiencing grief. And from that position, you have options. You can choose how you relate to the loss. You can choose what you do with the space that remains.

Meditation helps. Sitting quietly each morning and reminding yourself "I am the soul" doesn't make grief disappear, but it creates stability underneath it. You remember that you are not just the pain you're feeling. You are the eternal consciousness observing the pain, holding it, allowing it to be there without being consumed by it.

This is why spiritual understanding matters in grief. Not because it makes loss easier, but because it prevents despair. It keeps you from falling into hopelessness, from blaming yourself or others, from questioning the meaning of existence itself.

You lose someone you love. That's real. The space is empty. That's real. But they're not gone—not truly. The soul continues. The relationship continues. And you remain the soul, capable of transforming even this profound loss into something that deepens your capacity for love.

What Grief Teaches

Grief, faced with spiritual awareness, becomes a teacher.

It shows you how much you loved. How deeply you connected. How significant that person was to your consciousness and your life. These aren't small things. They're evidence of your own benevolent nature—your capacity for real relationship, real love, real impact.

Grief also shows you the truth about impermanence in physical form while revealing what's actually eternal. The body is temporary. Life in physical form is temporary. But consciousness continues. Love continues. Memory continues. Influence continues.

When you understand this, you begin to live differently. You realize that the time you have with people matters not because it will end, but because the relationship is actually eternal. What you create together, the love you share, the ways you influence each other—all of this lasts.

You become more present. More grateful. More willing to express love while people are still here in physical form.

And when they leave, you're not spared grief. But you're not destroyed by it either. Because you know something true: they're not gone. The space they occupied in your consciousness can become a place of continued connection, gratitude, and love.

Your benevolent nature—your capacity for compassion, kindness, love—shines through most clearly when you choose to transform grief into something that heals. Not by denying pain, but by meeting it with spiritual understanding and merciful self-observation.

You are a soul. Your nature is peace, love, benevolence. Even in grief, especially in grief, this remains true.

Points for Contemplation

When I remember someone who has passed, what feeling naturally arises? Can I allow it without judgment?

What space did this person occupy in my consciousness, and what lives there now?

Can I hold both grief and gratitude at the same time without forcing either?

If consciousness never dies, what does that mean about the people I've lost?

When memories arise, do I meet them with pain alone, or can I also send love?

What would it feel like to believe that my relationship with this person continues, just in a different form?

How does understanding myself as a soul change my experience of loss?

Confronting Anxiety

A NXIETY IS A PATTERN, a sanskar that lives in both mind and body. It can feel like chest pain, shortness of breath, tremors, the certainty that something terrible is about to happen. People rush to hospitals convinced they're having a heart attack, only to be told there's nothing wrong with their heart. The body is on fire with nerves. The mind floods with doom.

If you've experienced this, you know the helplessness it creates. The feeling that you've lost control, that something inside you has turned against you.

But here's what matters: the anxiety is not you. It's a pattern you're witnessing.

This distinction changes everything.

What Anxiety Actually Is

Anxiety runs in families. It's not a character flaw or a failure of willpower. It's a condition, like diabetes, a predisposition in the system that doesn't simply disappear because you want it to.

The mind creates fatalistic thinking, survival fears, racing catastrophic scenarios. The body responds with physical symptoms so real that people think they're dying. This mind-body synergy makes anxiety particularly convincing. It doesn't feel like just a thought or just a feeling. It feels like your entire system is under threat.

Understanding this matters because compassion begins with accuracy. You're not weak for having anxiety. You're dealing with a genuine condition that requires both care and courage.

The Two Sides of Response

There are moments when anxiety needs tenderness. You take medication if that's what helps. You see a therapist. You rest when your body asks for rest. You let someone sit with you through the storm.

This is the caring side, and it's necessary.

But there are also moments when anxiety needs to be confronted directly. Not with harshness, but with clarity. Not with self-criticism, but with spiritual authority.

This is where most people struggle. They know how to be kind to themselves, but they don't know how to be firm. They've learned to soothe their patterns but not to distinguish themselves from them.

Years ago, I boarded a plane for a thirteen-hour flight to India. I'd traveled the world alone before, but an hour into this flight, a massive panic attack hit. My energy spiked. My mind raced with terrifying thoughts. I felt completely out of control.

I was alone on that plane with nowhere to go. I considered my options. Talk to the flight attendant? They'd want to land the plane. I didn't want that. So I had to make a choice.

I'd been practicing meditation for years by then. I'd been learning that thoughts are just thoughts and emotions are just emotions. They're not me. In that moment, I decided to test whether I actually believed it.

I said to God: I'm going to do this and it's either going to work or it's not.

Then I started fighting in my mind. Nobody around me knew what was happening. But I was standing up to every thought, every wave of fear. You're just a thought. You're not real. You're just an emotion. You're not real.

I got through the flight. The anxiety lasted three more days, but I had a friend who helped me keep moving, keep getting dressed, keep showing up. And I told myself: if I get through this by standing up to it, it will never be this bad again.

It never was.

When to Be Kind and When to Be Firm

The caring side and the firm side aren't opposites. They're both forms of self-respect. You need to know which one a situation requires.

A friend once called me the morning of a flight to Europe. She'd missed the flight the day before because of anxiety. Now she'd rescheduled for that morning and was still in bed, frozen, unable to move.

When anxiety or depression freezes you, it's not laziness. It's the pattern asserting control.

I was firm with her. Get up. Get dressed. Go. If you don't go on this trip, this thing wins. Don't let it win. Take your medicine right now. Call me back in ten minutes.

I stayed with her all the way to the airport.

Sometimes people need someone to care for them gently. Sometimes they need someone to refuse to let them be defeated. The same is true in your relationship with yourself.

Anxiety wants to stop you from moving. One of the most practical things you can do is move anyway. Get up. Walk. Do the thing you said you'd do.

This isn't about forcing yourself through willpower. It's about recognizing that the pattern has no actual authority over you. You are the soul. The anxiety is a sanskar. And when you see that distinction clearly, you can act from your own nature rather than from the pattern.

The Foundation Beneath the Fight

The reason I could stand up to anxiety on that plane wasn't because I suddenly became strong. It was because I'd spent years in meditation practicing the distinction between consciousness and content.

Thoughts are just thoughts. Emotions are just emotions. The body does what it does. But I am the soul observing all of it.

This seems like a small thing until you're in the middle of a storm. Then it becomes everything.

When you practice meditation daily, you're training your intellect to recognize this distinction. You sit and tell yourself, "I am a soul, my nature is peace," and your mind wanders to errands or laundry. You notice. You bring it back. You're developing the capacity to witness rather than drown.

In moments of anxiety, that capacity becomes your lifeline. You're not trying to stop the thoughts or fix the emotions. You're simply refusing to be destroyed by them.

Living with the Pattern

I went six years without anxiety after that flight. Then it came back suddenly, out of nowhere. I went to therapy to understand why. The therapist told me it can return at any time.

That was when I finally accepted that this is a potential in my system. It may show up again. But now I have the tools. I know what to do.

I take care of myself. I meditate. I practice soul consciousness. And if medication becomes necessary again, I'll take it without shame. Right now I don't need it. The more I meditate, the less frequently anxiety appears.

The victory isn't in eliminating the condition. The victory is in gaining power within the situation. It's in knowing that no matter what the mind and body do, you remain yourself—the soul, the consciousness, the benevolent presence that was never actually threatened.

This is spiritual self-respect. Not pride in overcoming something, but the quiet dignity of knowing what you actually are.

When you get better, everyone around you gets better. When you stand up to your own patterns with clarity and mercy, you become someone others can turn to. Not because you're perfect, but because you've learned to distinguish yourself from what isn't you.

The benevolent nature was always there. Anxiety just blocked access to it. And now, through practice and courage, you're clearing the way.

Points for Contemplation

Where do I feel most helpless in my life? What pattern convinces me I have no power?

Do I know the difference between caring for myself and being firm with myself? Can I recognize which one a situation needs?

Have I truly distinguished myself from my thoughts and emotions, or do I still believe I am my anxiety?

What would it mean to stand witness to my most overwhelming feelings without being destroyed by them?

Am I willing to ask for help when I need it? Do I know who I can turn to?

When the pattern wants to freeze me or stop me from acting, can I move anyway?

What does it feel like to recognize: this is a sanskar, but I am the soul observing it?

Choosing Authenticity

G ROWING UP, I UNDERSTOOD happiness as something that happened to you when the right external conditions aligned. Your team won. You got the promotion. Someone said yes. The excitement was real, but it always faded, and then you were back where you started, looking for the next thing to feel good about.

I also learned that if you weren't succeeding at something, you couldn't possibly be happy doing it. I once watched people bowl and laugh through gutter ball after gutter ball, genuinely enjoying themselves despite failing repeatedly. That made no sense to me. How could they be having fun if they weren't winning?

Later, when I began meditating, my husband would tell me he was happy. He had a calm presence, a steadiness that seemed unshakeable. But when I asked where the happiness was, I genuinely couldn't see it. There was no excitement, no visible joy. Just this quiet contentment that felt completely foreign.

So I had two reference points for happiness: the excitement I knew but couldn't sustain, and the peaceful contentment I couldn't access or even recognize.

It turns out that neither of these was true.

What Authenticity Actually Means

The word authentic comes from the same root as authority. To be authentic is to have authority over yourself. Not power over others, not control over circumstances, but sovereignty over your own inner state.

When you tell the truth about where you are, something shifts. Not immediately into happiness, not into some elevated spiritual state, but into something more fundamental: self-respect.

I started meditating not because I felt peaceful but because I needed to stop lying to myself about how I actually felt. I was tired of performing, tired of comparing, tired of the constant internal pressure to be something I wasn't.

The first thing meditation taught me was to sit with what was actually true. I don't feel peaceful right now. I'm agitated. I'm worried. I'm pretending everything is fine when it isn't.

Just naming that reality created a foundation more stable than happiness. I could stand on the truth even when I couldn't stand on anything else.

If self-respect depends on circumstances going well, on other people responding positively, on achieving the next goal, it will constantly fluctuate. But if it's rooted in something internal, something you can always access regardless of what's happening around you, it becomes steady.

That internal foundation is authenticity. The capacity to know what's true for you and stand on it without apology.

Building Authority From Within

When you begin to practice merciful self-observation, you start seeing the patterns that have been running automatically. The comparing. The performing. The constant internal commentary about whether you're measuring up.

These are sanskars, impressions formed over time, and they've been convincing you that happiness depends on something external. But as you observe them rather than believe them, you realize:

You are not the pattern that says you need to achieve more to feel worthy. You are the consciousness observing that pattern.

You are not the comparison that tells you everyone else has figured something out that you haven't. You are the soul witnessing that thought arise and pass.

This distinction is what creates authentic self-respect. Not because you've become perfect or peaceful or anything else, but because you've stopped lying about where you actually are.

The truth, even when it's uncomfortable, is something you can stand on. And standing on truth builds self-respect in a way that chasing happiness never will.

The Soul's Authentic Nature

Here's what I've discovered through practice: I can't always be happy. I can't always be peaceful. I can't always be generous or patient or any of the other qualities I think I should embody.

But I can always be authentic. I can always tell the truth about what's actually happening.

And when I do that consistently, when I stop trying to force myself into some idea of what spiritual looks like and simply acknowledge what's real, something underneath begins to emerge.

It's not something I create. It's something that was there all along, waiting for the performance to stop so it could finally be recognized.

This is the benevolent nature of the soul. Not manufactured or achieved, but uncovered. Like rust being chipped away to reveal what was always beneath it.

The process isn't always comfortable. Each time you tell a truth you've been avoiding, each time you acknowledge a feeling you've been dismissing, there's a small death of the false self. The one who was trying so hard to be acceptable, to measure up, to achieve the right spiritual state.

But what remains is real. And real is better than performed.

When You Stop Faking It

There's a scene in the film *Eat Pray Love* where the main character puts on a badge indicating she's entering silence at an ashram. She's convinced this is what she needs, that silence will finally make her spiritual.

The moment she puts the badge on, the director asks her to greet and care for new visitors—a role perfectly suited to her talkative, welcoming personality. She takes the silence badge off, sets it on the table, and says, "I'm your girl."

Nobody can take away what you really are. So why not work with it instead of against it?

This doesn't mean your patterns and reactions don't need observation. It means the authentic you, the soul expressing through this particular personality, doesn't need to be fixed. It needs to be distinguished from everything you've been performing.

When you stop trying to be peaceful and start being honest, peace eventually arrives on its own. Not because you chased it, but because you cleared away what was blocking it.

The Practice of Truth

If you're standing somewhere right now thinking you should feel differently than you do, that you should be more peaceful, more happy, more spiritually advanced, consider this: what if that entire framework is what's keeping you from accessing what's real?

Try something different this week. Each morning in meditation, after you sit and remember your spiritual identity, ask yourself one question: what is actually true for me right now?

Not what should be true. Not what you wish were true. What *is* true.

Then observe what arises without trying to fix it or improve it. Just notice. Just witness.

This is how you begin to distinguish yourself from the patterns. You become the soul observing the sanskars rather than the bundle of sanskars hoping to feel better.

Happiness will come and go. Circumstances will shift. Moods will fluctuate. But the capacity to tell the truth and stand on it remains constant.

This is spiritual self-respect: the recognition that your benevolent nature doesn't depend on feeling a certain way. It depends on being willing to see what's real and work with it honestly.

The soul's nature is already peaceful. Already loving. Already wise. You're not trying to create these qualities. You're learning to stop blocking them with performance and pretense.

Your true nature doesn't need to be happy all the time. It just needs to be real, to be authentic.

Points for Contemplation

Where am I performing instead of being authentic?

What truth about myself have I been avoiding because I think I should feel differently?

When do I feel most like myself? What makes that possible?

If I gave myself permission to be exactly as I am right now, what would change?

What would it mean to build self-respect on truth rather than achievement?

4

Healing the Past

The Memory Trap

M OST OF US ASSUME that our responses in the present moment are responses to what's actually happening. Someone speaks to us, and we react. A situation unfolds, and we respond. But are we really responding to what's in front of us, or are we responding to what we've recorded about similar moments in the past?

This is the question at the heart of the memory trap.

Memory isn't the problem. We need memory to function. We need it to recognize faces, to speak, to know how to navigate our days. But if we aren't careful, memory stops being a tool and becomes a lens that distorts everything we see.

What Memory Actually Does

Memory is consciousness recording experience. Something happens in the physical world, and your consciousness captures it. The more emotional charge attached to the experience, the deeper it records. Joy, beauty, awe—these leave their mark. But pain, fear, humiliation? These etch themselves even more deeply.

There are three kinds of memory. Positive memories carry warmth, happiness, a sense of connection. Neutral memories are practical, like how to tie your shoes, how to drive, information you need to function. Then there are the negative memories, the ones that carry pain. And these, whether we realize it or not, record most easily of all.

You can live without memory in the technical sense. People with amnesia are alive. People with dementia are alive. The heart beats, the lungs breathe, the body functions without the mind's recordings. But to function as a human being in the world? For that, memory is essential.

The question isn't whether you need memory. The question is whether memory is running you.

When the Past Replaces the Present

The memory trap happens when you use past recordings to navigate present moments in ways that create negative outcomes. You respond not to what someone is actually saying, but to what someone said to you last week. You make decisions not based on what's actually available, but on what happened the last time you tried something similar.

Think about the last time someone at work didn't say hello when you walked in. Did you immediately wonder if they were upset with you? Did you start constructing a story about why they might not like you? That's the memory trap. Somewhere along the way, you recorded the idea that people who don't greet you don't like you. Now that recording plays automatically, whether it has anything to do with reality or not.

In spirituality, there's a word for this: Maya. Illusion. When you operate from a memory as though it's truth, as though it's real, you're living in illusion. The person who didn't say hello might have been preoccupied, might not have seen you, might have been having a difficult morning. But you're not responding to them. You're responding to your recording.

This is how memory becomes a trap. It's not appropriate to the moment. It's not cooperative. It's not based on what's actually happening.

The Recordings You Don't See

Some memories run so deep that you don't even realize they're operating. Post-traumatic stress, anxiety, and depression aren't just mental states. They're the result of experiences recorded so powerfully that they've embedded themselves in both mind and body. You might not even know why you feel the way you feel. But something from the past is determining how you experience now.

I once taught an online meditation class where one student came every week and said the same thing: "I don't know if this is for me. I really need something in person. I haven't been able to find anything. I don't know if I can meditate." Week after week, the same words. I kept encouraging: keep coming back, keep practicing. Maybe something will break through.

But the recording was louder than the encouragement. The person kept playing the same tape about themselves, about their capacity, about what they needed. Eventually, they stopped coming. The memory trap had won.

This is what happens when we live in our heads. The recordings play so loudly, feel so real, that we can't hear anything else. We can't hear encouragement. We can't see new possibilities. We respond to life from a script written years ago.

The Decisions That Limit Us

I learned to play golf as a teenager. I wasn't very good, and I felt humiliated. I decided right then: I'm never playing golf again. And I never did.

That's a small example, but look at what happened. I had one experience, one feeling, and I made a permanent decision. I cut myself off from something that might have brought joy, connection, opportunities to be with others. I limited my own life based on a single recording.

For me, the memory says: if I'm not doing well, I can't enjoy myself. So I show up stiff, unable to be spontaneous, maybe even a little negative about the whole thing. Who wants to be around that energy?

These aren't moral failures. But can you see how they limit life? How they affect the energy you bring into a room? How they make you less available to what's actually happening?

The memory trap means you're living in your recordings rather than in reality. And everyone around you feels it.

Seeing What's Running You

The first step out of the trap is observation. You have to see the patterns. You have to notice when you're responding to a recording instead of to what's in front of you.

This is where meditation becomes essential. When you sit quietly and say, "I am a soul, my nature is peace," your mind will immediately go somewhere else. To errands to be done. To tomorrow's meeting. To something someone said last week. You're watching the recordings play in real time.

Most people think of meditation as a way to calm down. And it does that. But the deeper purpose is distinction. You're learning to recognize: this is not me. This is a recording. I am the soul observing this pattern, not the pattern itself.

When I started Raja Yoga meditation, my anger disappeared in two weeks. Irritation and frustration took longer to distinguish myself from. But real anger, the kind that takes over? Gone. How did that happen? I started watching my mind. I started seeing where the anger came from. I started taking responsibility for what was recorded in my consciousness.

That's the shift. From being controlled by memory to witnessing it.

Taking Responsibility for Consciousness

Memory itself isn't good or bad. It's a function of being human. But you can be responsible for it. You can decide what gets recorded. You can work with the recordings that cause suffering.

There's a practice of going back into painful memories and rewriting them in your consciousness. Not to deny what happened, but to relieve yourself of the pain signal that keeps firing. You go back and give yourself what you needed. You make the person say what you needed to hear. You meet your own needs, even if only in your mind.

This isn't delusion. It's mercy. You're taking responsibility for your own consciousness, for what you carry, for how those recordings affect your life now.

The more you practice observing your mind, the more you'll notice these patterns. At first, it might not be pleasant. You'll see how often you're negative, how much you sabotage your own peace, how many limiting decisions you've made based on old recordings. But that seeing is the beginning of freedom.

You can't change what you can't see.

Points for Contemplation

What memories do I rely on that may not serve the present moment?

When do I notice myself responding to recordings rather than to what's actually happening?

What energy do I project when trapped in memory versus when present as the soul?

Which painful recording keeps playing? What happens when I observe it without becoming it?

Where have I made limiting decisions based on single experiences?

What would it feel like to be spontaneous, to respond from my benevolent nature rather than from my recordings?

Healing Family Wounds

F AMILY SITS AT THE center of human karma. These are the closest relationships we have in this world, the ones that shaped our earliest patterns, the ones we cannot simply walk away from even when we try. Blood is thicker than water, people say, as if proximity alone creates a permanent bond. And in a way, it does. Not because family members are bound by obligation, but because the soul has chosen these particular relationships as the primary laboratory for its own transformation.

The suffering we experience in family relationships isn't caused by the other person. It's revealed by them. They trigger something already present in us, some pattern we've been carrying, some way we learned to protect ourselves that no longer serves. The question isn't how to fix them or get them to change. The question is: what am I doing with my own energy in this relationship?

I spent years adjusting myself to match the emotional climate around me, trying to keep peace by becoming smaller. Or I moved in the opposite direction, judging everyone and trying to control the situation so I could feel safe. Both responses created the same result: I couldn't be myself. I wasn't free. And I subtly blamed my family for that lack of freedom.

The path to healing family wounds begins when you stop making them responsible for how you feel.

Why Family is the Spiritual Ground

Every culture holds beliefs about family. Some emphasize loyalty, others independence. Some see family as sacred duty, others as optional connection. Whatever the cultural frame, family represents the relationships where our patterns first formed and where they continue to play out with the most intensity.

Family members know which buttons to push because they installed most of them. The sensitivity you feel around certain people, the reactivity that appears nowhere else in your life, the old roles you slip back into the moment you walk through the door—all of this reveals where your work is.

From the soul's perspective, family relationships are not accidents. They are the karmic connections that offer the most direct path to self-knowledge. When you can remain peaceful in the presence of those who once destabilized you, you know something has shifted. Not in them. In you.

Self-Care as Creating Space

The first step in healing any family wound is to adopt an attitude of genuine self-care. Not the surface kind that looks like bubble baths and affirmations. The kind we explore in this book, the kind that requires you to examine where you've been giving your energy away without awareness.

Some people in my family have always had clear limits about what they would and wouldn't do, what they would and wouldn't tolerate. I thought that was selfish. I thought love meant being available for everything, sharing everything, helping with everything. What I didn't realize was that I was depleting myself and then resenting them for it.

Self-care means creating space between the soul and the sanskar. In this case, the sanskar is the automatic adjustment, the over-giving, the need to fix or control. The soul is the one who can observe that pattern without becoming it. When you create space, you give yourself room to see what's actually happening instead of just reacting to it.

This space can be physical: spending less time together until you feel steadier. It can be verbal: saying less, sharing less, keeping responses simple. It can be emotional: not taking on their feelings as your own, not making their reactions mean something about you. And it can be energetic: pulling back the constant outflow of attention and care that leaves you empty.

None of this is done with anger. If you're pulling back to punish someone or prove a point, that's not self-care. That's still reaction. Self-care is merciful. You're simply noticing where the exchange of energy has become unbalanced and making a quiet adjustment.

The Practice of Pulling Back

I had to learn to stop complaining. I thought sharing my grievances created connection, but it only created more negativity. I had to learn to stop over-sharing every detail of my struggles. When someone asked how I was, I started saying, "I'm great," and leaving it there. Not as a lie, but as a boundary. Not everything needs to be discussed.

I also had to stop over-giving. If someone needed something and I had other commitments, I learned to say, "I'm not able to do that." Not with explanation or apology. Just a simple statement of what was true. At first this felt impossible. The pattern of saying yes to everyone else and no to myself ran deep.

But each time I honored my own limits, something shifted. Self-respect began to return. I started to recognize what I actually needed and how to express it without apology. I learned that setting a boundary wasn't rejecting the other person. It was respecting both of us.

You'll know where you need boundaries by noticing where it hurts. Where you feel resentment, sadness, exhaustion, loss of control—those are the places where your energy has been flowing out without awareness. The work isn't to fix the relationship. The work is to observe your own patterns within it and begin to distinguish yourself from them.

Getting in Touch with Real Feelings

Underneath all the adjusting and fixing and controlling, there are real feelings you haven't been letting yourself experience. Anger, perhaps. Grief. Disappointment. Fear of rejection. Longing for connection that feels safe.

You cannot heal what you won't acknowledge. And you cannot acknowledge what you're constantly trying to manage away through behavior.

The red pill of karma is total self-responsibility. Not because you caused everything that happened to you, but because you're the only one who can transform your experience of it. No one else is coming to rescue you. No one else can give you permission to feel what you feel or change what you've been doing.

This requires mercy toward yourself. When you notice how much you've been over-giving, the response isn't self-criticism. The response is understanding. Of course you did that. You were trying to feel safe, trying to be loved, trying to maintain connection in the only way you knew how. The pattern made sense. It just doesn't serve you anymore.

As you sit in meditation and observe these patterns, you'll begin to see them for what they are: sanskars, not your true nature. You are the soul watching the mind replay old strategies. Each time you can observe without identification, the pattern loses a little power. You stop suffering from it even when it still appears.

Karma gives you repeated opportunities to practice. If you try to set a boundary and it comes out with anger, there will be another chance. If you pull back too far and isolate yourself, you'll notice and can adjust. This isn't a test you pass or fail. It's an investigation you deepen over time.

The Transformation of Energy

As you continue this work, something unexpected happens. The relationships themselves begin to shift, not because the other person changed but because your energy within the relationship has transformed.

When you stop over-giving, you stop creating resentment. When you stop complaining, you stop feeding negativity. When you stop trying to fix everyone, you create space for them to be exactly as they are. And in that space, something new becomes possible: genuine respect.

This is what spiritual self-respect looks like in action. You recognize your own benevolent nature and you protect it by managing your energy wisely. You recognize that each person in your family is also a soul, also carrying sanskars, also doing the best they can with what they know. You don't need them to change for you to be at peace.

I won't tell you that every family relationship can be healed to the point of closeness. Some relationships require permanent distance. Some patterns run too deep, some wounds remain too raw. But even in those cases, you can heal your side of the equation. You can stop blaming, stop waiting for apologies, stop giving away your power to people who cannot or will not meet you differently.

What I can tell you is that transformation is real. I have witnessed it in my own family. Relationships I thought were permanently damaged have become sources of genuine connection. People I couldn't be in the same room with are now people I can sit beside with ease. Not because they changed everything about themselves, but because I changed my relationship to my own patterns.

As you become more calm, more self-respecting, more clear about your boundaries, you serve everyone around you. Your family benefits from your transformation even if they never understand what you're doing. The spiritual vibration you carry when you're living from soul consciousness affects every interaction.

Points for Contemplation

What are the ways I typically respond to family stress?

What would self-care actually look like in one specific family relationship right now?

Can I identify a real feeling I haven't been letting myself fully experience?

Where am I still blaming someone else for how I feel, and what would it mean to take that responsibility back?

Can I bring an attitude of mercy to my own history of coping, recognizing that I was doing the best I knew how?

Releasing the Past

T HERE'S A SAYING THAT people don't remember what you said, they remember how you made them feel.

This is true for our own memories as well. When you think of your childhood, what comes first? Probably not the specific words spoken at dinner or the exact sequence of events. What comes is a feeling. Safety or anxiety. Warmth or loneliness. Belonging or isolation.

The details fade. The essence remains.

This distinction matters because when we try to release the past, we often focus on the wrong thing. We try to forget incidents, erase memories, stop thinking about what happened. But the mind doesn't work that way. The more you push against a memory, the more present it becomes.

What actually needs attention is the feeling beneath the memory, the essence you've been carrying in your heart.

Notice this for yourself. When you recall something painful, observe how many thoughts arise. The mind generates endless details, interpretations, what should have happened, what could have been different. But when you recall something peaceful, the experience is simpler. There's a feeling, a quality, without all the mental elaboration.

The heart remembers essence. The mind creates stories about it.

The Practice of Merciful Review

Here's what actually works: you can choose what to keep.

Not through force or willful forgetting, but through honest reflection. You look at a period of your life and ask: what is the essence I want to carry forward? What feeling, what quality, what understanding do I want to preserve?

This isn't about pretending everything was perfect. It's about distinguishing what matters from what doesn't.

Consider dividing your life into natural stages. Childhood, teenage years, young adulthood, career, relationships, whatever divisions feel true for you. Then for each stage, ask yourself: what do I want to remember about this time?

When I did this for my teenage years, the answer that came was music. I spent every free moment at the piano, singing, creating. The feeling was happiness, self-expression, belonging. That's what I want to keep. Not every awkward interaction or disappointment, but that quality of joy and creative freedom.

From childhood, what came was my relationship with my sister. We were so close that even now, when I speak about that time, I say "we" automatically. The essence I want to preserve is that feeling of closeness, of sharing life with someone, of never being alone.

From my nursing career, what matters is the intention to help, the willingness to be an instrument for healing. That quality of service, of putting myself in position to care for others.

Look at those three essences: togetherness, creative joy, service. If that's what I carried forward from those entire periods of my life, releasing all the painful details and unnecessary complexity, wouldn't that be enough? Wouldn't that be beautiful?

The practice is simple but requires honesty. You're not manufacturing positive memories or denying what was difficult. You're making a conscious choice about what deserves space in your heart moving forward.

What Continues Beyond the Body

There's a spiritual principle that clarifies why this matters so deeply.

When we leave the body, when we pass on, all the details are finished. The circumstances, the relationships, the specific events, all of it remains behind. But what's in the heart continues. What you've been holding as your felt truth about your life, that's what moves forward with you.

This is why cultures create memorial rituals. When someone dies, we gather and remember them. We speak about what they meant to us, the qualities they embodied, the feelings they inspired. We're helping that person's essence crystallize, both for ourselves and for them.

We can do this for ourselves while we're still here.

Why wait? Why carry the weight of every painful detail, every regret, every should-have-been when you could choose now to hold only what matters?

This isn't spiritual bypassing. It's spiritual maturity. You're not pretending the difficult things didn't happen. You're recognizing that you don't need to carry them in your heart anymore.

The Soul's Capacity to Release

As the soul observing your life, you have a capacity the mind doesn't possess. You can witness your entire history without being overwhelmed by it.

The mind wants to analyze, justify, hold grudges, replay scenarios. But the soul simply observes and asks: what is true? What matters? What do I want to preserve?

When you practice this kind of review, you're strengthening your identity as the soul rather than as your accumulated experiences. You're learning to distinguish yourself from your story.

This is how you develop the power to put a full stop, to move cleanly from one scene to the next without dragging everything behind you. The excessive thinking stops because you're no longer identified with the details. You're holding essence instead.

Notice how this changes your relationship to the present moment. When your heart isn't crowded with painful histories, when you're carrying only what's meaningful, you have space to actually be here. The past no longer colonizes now.

This is what it means to live from soul consciousness rather than from your sanskars. You're not controlled by accumulated patterns. You're choosing, with clarity and mercy, what continues and what ends.

An Invitation to Begin

You don't need to review your entire life at once. Start with one period, one relationship, one significant experience.

Sit quietly. Let yourself remember, not the details but the quality of that time. Ask yourself honestly: what do I want to keep? What feeling, what understanding, what essence actually serves me?

Then let yourself release the rest. Not through effort, but through choice. You're distinguishing what matters from what doesn't. You're practicing benevolent observation and discernment.

Some periods you'll return to multiple times. The first time you might identify one quality to preserve. Later, you might see something deeper, a more essential truth. This is natural. You're excavating your own heart with increasing clarity.

The goal isn't to create a sanitized version of your past. The goal is to free yourself from carrying what you don't need while honoring what's genuinely meaningful.

The past you carry in your heart shapes your present. Choose carefully what you keep.

Points for Contemplation

Am I ready to distinguish between the details of my past and the essence I want to preserve?

What period of my life still feels heavy when I think about it? What feeling am I carrying from that time?

If I could keep only three qualities from my entire life so far, what would they be?

Can I observe my own history with the merciful curiosity of the soul rather than the judgment of the mind?

What is my heart actually asking me to release?

Creating My Future

CONSIDER WHAT YOU SAY you want. Maybe it's a specific job, a certain income, a relationship that looks a particular way. But if you look beneath those stated desires, what are you actually seeking? Often it's not the thing itself but the experience you believe the thing will give you.

I once thought I wanted a leadership position at work. I pursued it, prepared for it, genuinely believed that role would give me what I was looking for. I didn't get it. But later I found myself in a different position where I had exactly what I'd actually wanted: meaningful impact, creative influence, the ability to shape practice in my field. The form was different. The experience was what mattered.

This is how spiritual creation works. You don't force outcomes. You create the inner conditions where what you truly desire can emerge naturally.

The Ground of Creation

Creation is already happening. Your life is being shaped by the energy you carry inside, by what you believe about yourself, by the patterns running beneath your awareness. So the most important consideration is: what quality of consciousness are you creating from?

When the inner ground is cluttered with false identifications, old wounds, unexamined beliefs about worthiness, what emerges reflects that clutter. When the inner ground is clear, when you're standing in your actual nature as a soul, what emerges reflects that clarity.

This is why purification matters. Not to make yourself better, but to see what's true. To distinguish yourself from what you've been carrying that was never you.

Four Territories of Inner Clearing

There are four areas that need honest examination if you want to create from a clear place.

Who do I think I am?

The first territory is identity itself. Most of us think we are what we do, where we're from, what we've accomplished or failed at. We identify with nationality, profession, family role, past mistakes. All of this limits what feels possible.

Meditation reverses this. You sit quietly and remember: I am a soul. My original nature is peace. This isn't philosophy. It's the basic distinction that changes everything. When you know you are the consciousness observing the mind rather than the contents of the mind, you become unlimited.

What do I think I deserve?

The second territory is worthiness. Whatever religious or cultural background shaped you, chances are you absorbed some version of unworthiness. Standards you couldn't meet.

181

Judgments you internalized. A sense that you're not quite good enough, that real happiness belongs to other people.

I worked with a student once who struggled to feel he was making good spiritual effort. Every time he tried, memories of past mistakes would surface. He couldn't let them go, couldn't forgive himself, couldn't believe he was capable of real transformation. The judgments he carried cut him off from his own benevolent nature.

This is where honest examination becomes essential. Question what you believe about your worthiness. Are you still measuring yourself against standards that were never about truth? Can you face what happened, acknowledge it honestly, and choose to move forward? Can you forgive yourself?

You cannot create a future you don't believe you deserve. This layer has to be cleared.

Who am I in relation to others?

The third territory is how you experience yourself with other people. Your self-esteem, your sense of satisfaction, your feeling of success may all be tangled up in these relationships.

Look around. How do you feel about your family? Your colleagues? Are you satisfied with those connections? If not, what's actually happening? Comparison? Jealousy? A need for validation? Resentment?

This isn't about fixing relationships. It's about seeing your part clearly. When you change, when you shift the energy you bring, others shift too. At first they may react because the familiar pattern has changed. But eventually, what's genuine finds its level.

What do I really want?

The fourth territory is desire itself. Beneath what you think you want, what is the actual experience you're seeking?

Maybe you say you want to be married. But what you really want is security. Or companionship. Or to build a family. The form and the experience aren't the same thing.

I notice even now that I sometimes feel nervous saying what I truly want. Old habits surface, whispers that suggest if I show myself fully, something bad will happen. I'm not alone in this. Most of us have learned to hide our real desires, even from ourselves.

But this is where creation actually happens. When you can name what you truly want, not the surface goal but the heart experience, you begin to align with it. You create space for it to emerge.

The Practice of Merciful Looking

This isn't a one-time inventory. It's an ongoing practice of honest self-reflection. You sit with each territory and simply observe. Who do I think I am today? What do I believe I deserve? How am I experiencing my relationships? What am I actually wanting?

The looking itself is purifying. When you observe without judgment, patterns begin to loosen. You start to distinguish yourself from them. I am not this belief about unworthiness. I am the soul observing that I've been carrying it.

The key is mercy. You're not attacking yourself for what you find. You're investigating with genuine curiosity. What's actually here? Where did this come from? Is it true?

Your intellect becomes your ally in this work. The awakened intellect can see patterns clearly and guide you back to what's real. I am a soul. My nature is peace, love, benevolence, wisdom. When the intellect holds this truth steady, the patterns begin to release naturally.

When Desire Becomes Benevolent

At first you're looking at your own desires, clearing the ground so what you really want can emerge. But as purification continues, your desires themselves begin to change.

You start wishing things for others. Not in an artificial way, but genuinely. I want my father to be happy. I want resolution for my sister. I want this person to feel at peace. The wish arises naturally from a place of generosity.

This is how you know you're accessing your benevolent nature. Real creativity comes from here. Real attraction comes from here. When you're standing in your authentic self, when your desires reflect your actual nature as a soul, something radiates outward that others can sense.

You're no longer forcing or manipulating. You're simply being what you are, and what you are is naturally creative, naturally generous, naturally attractive in the spiritual sense.

This work doesn't create something new. It reveals what was already present but couldn't express through all the accumulated clutter.

Your benevolent nature was always there. Your wisdom was always there. Your capacity for genuine love and compassion was always there. You just couldn't access it through the false identifications, the worthiness wounds, the relationship distortions, the hidden desires.

As you clear each layer with honest observation, the authentic self begins to shine through. Not as something you've constructed, but as what you've always been beneath the patterns.

This is spiritual creation. Not planning outcomes or forcing circumstances, but purifying the inner ground so your true nature can express freely. When that happens, your life begins to reflect who you actually are. The gap between your inner experience and your outer life closes.

You're not becoming someone different. You're becoming yourself. And from that place, everything you create carries the quality of your soul: peaceful, loving, wise, benevolent, pure.

The future you're creating isn't separate from who you are. It's the natural expression of consciousness that knows itself clearly.

Points for Contemplation

Who do I think I am beneath the roles and identifications I carry?

What beliefs about worthiness am I still holding that limit what feels possible?

What do I say I want, and what is the actual experience I'm seeking beneath that?

What would it feel like to create from a place of knowing I am a soul, inherently benevolent and whole?

Where in my life am I already experiencing alignment between my inner nature and outer expression?

Author's Note

CONGRATULATIONS TO ALL OF you who have made it this far. My hope is that you have gained invaluable insights into how consciousness works from your own unique perspective, and also tasted your own benevolent nature.

The practices in this book are meant to continue for the rest of our lives; as we continue to grow in our depth of understanding and capacity for spiritual love.

If you are ready for more, please join me in the next book in this series, "Meditate for Everyone: Activating your Benevolent Nature." Here we will focus on changing our view of self, others, nature, and the world, into an unlimited view that is in alignment with natural laws and in harmony with all souls, all of nature, and all circumstances. This is the source of true self-respect, and is the birthright of every human being.

Love and blessings to each and every one of you on your continued journey.

Acknowledgements

To my Beloved Father, Mother, Teacher, Guide, Friend... my Everything. To the One who, when I remember, I cannot create words from the depth of love and respect that I feel. My heart fills with happiness and gratitude, my eyes fill with tears of love and appreciation. You are the most Beautiful One, the Creator, the Beloved of all souls and of Nature. Your mark is on the heart and mind of each and every soul, and every soul will receive unique fulfillment from You at the accurate time.

To Brahma Baba, Mama, and all the Brahma Kumaris original jewels and senior Didis whose extraordinary faith and sacrifice continue to provide support for the world and spiritual sustenance for us all.

To the worldwide BK Family who bravely and tirelessly strive everyday to purify the self and serve the world with love and powerful remembrance of One.

To my own family with love and gratitude. Whatever success I have is also yours.

About The Author

Anne O'Hare has been a lifelong student and spiritual aspirant. She has enjoyed a full life including marriage, a child, and a satisfying career in Nursing in which she holds a Doctorate of Nursing Practice in Leadership. She has been a student and teacher in The Brahma Kumaris since 2011. This worldwide spiritual movement values purity, ongoing spiritual effort, and surrender for service. She has dedicated her life to serving the United States in particular; sharing the message of universal access to spiritual knowledge and soul conscious experiences. Through Raja Yoga meditation practice and study, she encourages readers and podcast listeners to overcome the self-defeating forces within; courageously facing their mind to bring about healing, empowerment, and an emergence of their innate benevolent nature.

Connect with Dr. Anne: dr.anne.ohare@gmail.com

Listen to the Podcast: https://thespiritualamerican.com/

HEAL • EMPOWER • SERVE